Reading Emptiness

SUNY series, The Margins of Literature
Mihai I. Spariosu, Editor

Reading Emptiness

Buddhism and Literature

Jeff Humphries

State University of New York Press

COVER ART: Tosa Mitsuoki, Japanese, 1617–1691. Autumn Maple with Poem Slips, six-fold screen; ink, colors, gold leaf and powdered gold on silk, Edo period, c. 1675, 142.5 × 293.2 cm. Kate S. Buckingham Collection, 1977.157 (detail), photograph by Christopher Gallagher © 1998 The Art Institute of Chicago.

Published by
State University of New York Press, Albany

For information, address
State University of New York Press, State University Plaza, Albany, NY, 12246

Production by Dale Cotton and Michael Haggett
Marketing by Fran Keneston

Library of Congress Cataloging-in-Publication Data
Humphries, Jefferson, 1955-
        Reading emptiness : Buddhism and literature / Jeff Humphries.
            p.   cm.—(SUNY series, the margins of literature)
        Includes bibliographical references and index.
        ISBN 0-7914-4261-6 (hardcover : alk. paper).—ISBN 0-7914-4262-4
(pbk. : alk. paper)
            1. Buddhist literature—Philosophy.   2. Buddhism and literature.
3. Sunyata.   4. Hearn, Lafcadio, 1850–1904—Criticism and
interpretation.   I. Title.   II. Series.
BQ1020.H86   1999
294.3'375—dc21   98-47569
                                                           CIP

10 9 8 7 6 5 4 3 2 1

For Ann Kathryn Benjamin Humphries

Contents

Preface

This is not so much a work of scholarship or of criticism as a narrative in the form of an essay comprising several parts that are also essays, each of which calls on the resources of scholarship, criticism, literary theory and philosophy, and sometimes science. Its voice and its point of view are frankly personal and idiosyncratic. Part 1, comprising three chapters, is devoted to speculations about a possible common ground between literary and Buddhist practices, so I have called it "anti-theoretical," for lack of a better term. In fact its conclusions undermine and even dispense with theory as that term has been understood in the literary precincts of recent academe. Part 2, which examines the life and writing of Lafcadio Hearn, and the place of Buddhism in it, is a "defense and illustration" of the (anti-)theory elaborated previously. Any of the chapters could be read independently of the others, but read in sequence, each has a greater cumulative effect than if read alone.

I am not a specialist in Eastern religion or Eastern languages but a teacher and practitioner of literature. American universities now include among their faculties such remarkable scholars of Buddhism as Robert Thurman and Jeffrey Hopkins (and increasingly now their students), who have studied the traditions from within as well as without. I have neither their knowledge nor their scholarly apparatus at my disposal. But my purpose is quite different from theirs: not to elucidate the ancient traditions of Buddhism to Westerners but, using their work as a guide, to seek ways in which literature might be integrated into a truly Western practice of Buddhism that would remain true to its Eastern roots.

The bibliography reflects a mix of scholarly, "popular," and "devotional" literature, from "New Age" icons such as Alan Watts and Alexandra David-Neel to the most careful and recondite scholarship, to works by Tibetan lamas living in exile in the West. None has been used indiscriminately or without regard for its limits; each has its place here. Every effort has been made to guide the interested reader toward other sources of information. I have quoted only from translated sources that are readily available in most large libraries, and I have tried to be careful about which translations I have used. Every effort has been made to keep arcane vocabulary to a minimum.

My hope is that the book may offer one answer to the questions I am most often asked by students: why and how should they take literature seriously.

Two chapters of this book have appeared before, in very different versions: chapter 1 in *Southwest Review* (autumn 1994, vol. 79, no. 4), and chapter 3 in *University of Toronto Quarterly* (summer 1997, vol. 66, no. 3).

J. H.
Baton Rouge, Louisiana
March 1999

Introduction

This is not a Buddhist "theory" of literature. There cannot be such a thing, if as Nagarjuna wrote, "The emptiness of the conquerors was taught in order to do away with all philosophical views. Therefore it is said that whoever makes a philosophical view out of 'emptiness' is indeed lost" (Huntington, 3). However, neither the Buddha nor Nagarjuna ever said that texts, language, and literature could not contribute to enlightenment, to the direct apprehension of the nature of reality— though most Buddhists today seem to think that they did. Zen in particular is deeply corrupted by this misapprehension, in Japan as well as the West, though its Japanese founder, Dogen, was not (as I will show in the pages that follow). In an introduction to a key text by Nagarjuna, David Kalupahana writes that "in the Buddha's view language is not, in itself, an inadequate means of expressing what is empirically given. Yet modern interpreters of Buddhism seem to assume that the Buddha considered language inadequate to express the truth about existence that he discovered" (17). In fact, Kalupahana points out, the Buddha regarded language as a convention, and

> the difficulty lies in adopting a middle path without accepting conventions as being ultimate or rejecting them as being useless. The uniqueness of the Buddha's philosophy lies in the manner in which a middle path can be adopted with regard to any convention, whether it be linguistic, social, political, moral, or religious. (p. 18)

A classic Chinese text points out the ease, rather than the difficulty, of the Middle Path:

> All forms and appearances are stamped by impressions of a single reality; whatever you encounter [including language, and books] is real. . . . "Sentient beings" [conventional reality] and the "reality-body" [the reality of emptiness] are one in substance but different in name. There has never been movement or stillness, and no concealment or revelation. Because the names are different, there is

mutual interidentification, there is mutual concealment and can-
cellation; because they are one substance, they can interidentify
and can conceal and reveal each other. Because of this interidentification the two truths, real and conventional, have never been
contradictory. (Cleary, *Entry into the Inconceivable*, pp. 105–6)

In other words, the literary, along with every other sort of conventional
reality, is not different from the ultimate reality of emptiness. Thus to
the extent that it refuses to admit literature into the circle of right practice, contemporary Buddhism is missing an invaluable aspect of Buddhist teaching, the same aspect that also makes Buddhist thought invaluable to students and practitioners of literature.

   Part of the purpose of this book is to correct the misunderstanding
and prejudice against literature among Buddhists themselves, but in a
larger sense it is intended to provide some relief from a particularly
troublesome aspect of every Western theory of literature: the tendency
to consider a human reading a book as an animate, sentient thing (a
"thinking reed") confronting an inanimate, nonthinking thing—two objects, one endowed with the power of thought (a subject), both having
real, inherent existence. This view reflects both the tendency to reification, to consider things as objectively real, and the corollary tradition of
dualistic thought in the West since ancient times. That dualism is characteristic of both Platonic idealism and of empiricist materialism—two
sides of one coin. Monism—the view of Spinoza and Parminides that
everything is "one"—is dualistic in its own way, arising in opposition to
dualism, with which it makes a pair. Even the most radical Western
thinkers, from Nietzsche to Derrida, have had to operate within the context of a fundamental dualism. Reader-response theory is grounded in
the idea of the reader as agent, as subject, and of the text as object,
though defined in different terms than the traditional ones, without any
absolute or permanent characteristics. Deconstruction, in the person of
Jacques Derrida, thinks and writes from the vantage point of the ultimate *sujet supposé savoir*, the highly (over-)refined Cartesian subject-
who-is-supposed-to-know who knows that what he is supposed to
know is not what it is supposed to be (a static, reified "truth" or "thing"),
having only perceived and even deeply understood the phenomenon of
emptiness *in the object*. This position halfway in and halfway out of Cartesian dualism imbues deconstructionist discourse with both a gleeful,
deliberate obscurantism and a mournful heaviness, an existential angst,
which may both be unnecessary (see chapter 3). Despite his real insights

into the nature of conventional reality, Derrida finally goes no further than a recondite academic discourse, a playground for the effete post-romantic intellect. Of all Western streams of thought, the Buddhist Mad-hyamika is probably closest to Richard Rorty's pragmatism, with its emphasis on *phronesis* (practical wisdom), as opposed to *theoria*, which strives after only absolute, abstract truths.[1] In the Hua-yen tradition it is written that

> "Even if all sentient beings attain enlightenment in an instant, that is no different from not attaining enlightenment. Why? Because enlightenment has no forms or formlessness." Everything being formless, the noumenon thus is manifest—"sentient beings" and "Buddha" both vanish. (Cleary, *Entry into the Inconceivable*, p. 103)

This is the radical pragmatism or "everydayness" of Buddhism. Still, there are differences, starting with the fact that Rorty's pragmatism is at least provisionally subject-centered; it assumes the inherent reality of the subject, the agent of pragmatism.

From a point of view opposite to that of all Western literary theories, I wish to propose here that a human reading a book is a case of two entities, neither of which has any reified, static or inherent existence, involved in a process of mutual "projection." We are used to considering the book as a kind of lens, or mirror, that throws us back our searching look after effecting inflections or distortions, so that we don't recognize it as our own. Consider book and reader now as two mutually reflecting sets of lenses or mirrors, as mutually involved phenomena, one comprising perhaps only one lens, the other several, with this distinction of single on one side and multiple on the other being subject to constant and unpredictable reversal:

> One phenomenon is relative to all; there is inclusion, there is entry, with four steps in all; one includes all, one enters all; all include one, all enter one; one includes one phenomenon, one enters one phenomenonon; all include all, all enter all. They commune simultaneously without interference. . . .
>
> If we use the example of ten mirrors (arrayed in a circle or sphere so that all face all the others) as a simile, one mirror is the one, nine mirrors are the many. As the first expression states, "one includes all, one enters all," we should say that one mirror

includes in it (reflections of) nine mirrors, meaning that one mirror is that which includes and nine mirrors are that which is included—yet because the nine mirrors also are that which includes (because they contain the reflection of the one mirror), the aforementioned one mirror which includes also enters the nine mirrors, so one mirror enters nine mirrors. The next three expressions follow this pattern. The second expression says, "all include one, all enter one"—we should say that nine mirrors include in them one mirror, nine mirrors enter one mirror. That is to say, the first-mentioned nine mirrors are that which includes, so the one mirror is that which is included; because the included one also includes, the aforementioned including nine mirrors enter the one mirror, so nine mirrors enter one mirror. As for the third expression "one includes one thing, one enters one thing," we would say that one mirror includes one mirror, one mirror enters one mirror. This means that the first one mirror includes in it (the reflection of) a second one mirror, and the (reflection of the) first one mirror also enters the second one mirror. As for the fourth expression which says "all include all, all enter all," we would say that the ten mirrors each include in them (reflections of) nine mirrors, and (reflections of) ten mirrors all enter nine mirrors. That the entered and the included are only said to be nine mirrors is to leave one to include and enter. (Cleary, *Entry into the Inconceivable*, pp. 119–20)

Less abstractly, consider the book as though it were a raw oyster, tasting you as you taste it, but without being consumed in the process, or rather both consumed and not consumed at the same time. Not only is the "other" unknowable, as William James asserted, but it is not even really there at all, and not only that, but neither is the self, the would-be knower. This need not, however, and does not prevent human being from going on, or knowing things, including other beings, or reading. Nor is it in any sense tragic or pathetic, though to James and to Proust, and to every Western thinker, including Nietzsche—who merely transmuted his anguish into a lunatic grin—it has seemed wrenchingly so. Within the very limited domain in which they occur, these ways of knowing are perfectly valid, and even "true." The Buddhist Madhyamika or Middle Path does however discredit any effort to render these into any sort of permanent coherence, to understand them as having permanent or ultimate reality—despite whatever impressive material products may result.

Our empiricist science in the West has produced a remarkable capacity for manipulating material reality, but not much understanding of its nature, or of our connection to it. The same can be said for our theories of reading: they have produced remarkably sophisticated strategies and models for textual production, each with its own unique and exclusive claims to Truth, each with its own inadequacies, all the result of being grounded in an absolutist dualism: the reader is an object endowed with thought, and is the agent of knowing (the subject); the book is the inanimate object of inquiry.

That neither should be an object, and neither have any reified existence, as I propose following the philosophy of the Madhyamika, is not completely alien to Western modes of thinking; we need not sacrifice all of the latter to embrace it. On the contrary, it has affinities with the thought of many Western writers, including Montaigne, Proust, Derrida, Rorty, Wittgenstein, and Heidegger. One interpreter of Heidegger has paraphrased him by saying that human existence is "weird" because "humans are not things but the clearing in which things appear" (Zimmerman, p. 244). But this does not go far enough. *Books are the clearing in which human being appears, at least when human beings read.* Because our responses to them are out of all proportion to books as objects—what we "read" in them bears no relation to the paper and ink that are the book—the act of reading seems to be an exceptional instance of human being. In fact it is not exceptional, but exemplary. We are always seeing things that are not there, and we are in fact ourselves something that is not there, being seen by ourselves, and others, and even by books (which do not, it is true, see with eyes but with ink and paper, with words). This is not a mystical or even a paradoxical statement. My point here is not to mystify or proselytize but to articulate a different way of looking at texts that has profoundly affected my own readings, and allowed me to appreciate literature more.

I propose that no two texts can be fundamentally alien to each other; still, it is possible to argue, as some have done, that Western literature and Eastern thought are mutually exclusive. Despite affinities that may exist with Western thought, Buddhist philosophy does call deeply into question the most fundamental assumptions of the West about language and representation. It is a commonplace of Western linguistic theory since Saussure that the relation of sign to referent is completely arbitrary, that there is nothing beyond convention and artifice that links the two. This assumption grounds all of Derrida's thought, the entire intellectual edifice of deconstruction. And yet it is quite moot from the perspective of the Madhyamika. The sign can only be arbitrary if we imagine the thing existing on its own quite apart from our naming it, thinking it. Without inherence, without reified being, no thing can exist in this way. And every thing must become indistinguishable from our representations of it, from our words for it, our thoughts about it. Words (or mathematical formulas, if we are talking about the sciences) and the things they represent are like books and readers, mutually reflecting mirrors in the famous simile of Hua-yen Buddhism cited above—each appears within the other.

Even more basic, the distinction between nature and artifice has no place in Buddhist thought. Or rather, it only exists in reality to the extent that it exists in our minds. The distinction itself is only a convention, a delusion if we cannot see beyond it. The work of Francois Jullien has demonstrated that in much of Eastern intellectual and religious tradition, not only Buddhism, human culture is seen as an extension of nature, and language and art as "unfurling" from nature rather than arising in opposition to it. Both we, and literature, are part of the natural world. Books, words, thoughts can—and do, constantly—profoundly affect not just the way things are conceived, but their very nature. This implies a much greater responsibility toward the natural world, from which we can no longer separate ourselves. It also means that we must begin to take language, literature, textuality, much more seriously than we have been accustomed to do.

If this seems a frightening prospect to historians and journalists, so be it. Western journalism and history, like all the "empirical" disciplines, have grounded themselves in a deference to objective "fact," and to the subject/reader's need/desire to know those facts ("Inquiring minds want to know!"). Buddhist thought implies that there are no such things as facts entirely distinct from our representation of them, or from those to whom we represent them. So the value of disseminating information must be combined with, not compromised by, concern for the way in which the dissemination affects the information. This is different from censorship and propaganda, which are only concerned with the effect of information on an audience, and do not question the status of the information or the facts that it purports to represent. I am talking here about involvement and responsibility, not manipulation. We are wont to talk in the West about communication, whether in self-help books or scientific journals, as though we could talk about a fact or a situation without affecting it. We remain wedded to such misapprehensions even though empirical science (in the person of Werner Heisenberg, author of the Uncertainty Principle, and others besides him since) has discovered that they do not work. Even those in the West who have been most forcefully exposing the contradictory underpinnings of Western thought (Derrida, Foucault) remain firmly within these objectivist fallacies. If objects and facts cannot be studied as though existing independently of the study, neither can "discourses."

Obviously, I do not believe that Western literature and Buddhist thought cannot be mixed. The *Flower Ornament Scripture*, the principal scripture of the Hua-yen school of Buddhism, contains the following passage that I consider the cornerstone of this small book.

> "The nature of all sentient beings is naturelessness; the nature of all phenomena is uncreated; the form of all lands of formlessness—in all worlds there only exists verbal expression, and verbal expression has no basis in facts. Furthermore, facts have no basis in words." Thus do enlightening beings understand that all things are void, and all worlds are silent: all the Buddha teachings add nothing—the Buddha teachings are no different from the phenomena of the world, and the phenomena of the world are no different from the Buddha teachings. The Buddha teachings and worldly phenomena are neither mixed up nor differentiated. (p. 462)

The "Middle Way" or Madhyamika system of thought that is emphasized here rejects all theories, and all rationalism. At the same time, it embraces each as true on its own. And true without relativism, without regard to any other or higher "truth," of which there is none. The accusation of relativism reflects an absolutist assumption that if one truth is not absolutely true, another must be better, and some one must be the best one. Why should this be so? In Madhyamika Buddhist thought,

> The way of thinking and speaking that finds expression in propositions embodying epistemological and ontological claims is diagnosed as symptomatic of an extremely serious "mental affliction" (*klesa*), the generative force behind an inordinate and ultimately painful clinging to the "I" and to the objects used to insure the continued well-being of this "I." The Madhyamika maintains, moreover, that philosophers are not the only ones bound up so tightly in the web of reified thinking. In articulating these ideas of "necessary connection" and the like they merely reveal to public

scrutiny what is for the average person a clandestine, unconscious, and deeply engrained tendency of conceptual thought, that both generates and sustains an attitude and a pattern of behavior tainted by clinging, antipathy, and delusion. (Huntington, p. 55)

For the absolutist—and virtually all Western thinkers are absolutists, including those whose absolute embraces relativity—this raises the question: What room does this leave for words, or for theories, of any kind? The Indian Buddhist philosopher and interpreter of Nagarjuna, Candrakirti, answered as follows:

The problem of a connection between argument and counterargument is only a problem for those who presuppose some form of absolute, as you do, and are therefore compelled to meet your claims with appropriate counterclaims. For us it is a pseudoproblem, because we hold no such presuppositions. Our words are like the reflection of a face in a mirror—there is no real connection between the reflected image and the face, but the image nevertheless serves a specific purpose for the person using the mirror. Similarly, our words bear no intrinsic connection with your epistemological and ontological problems and the language used to express these problems, but nevertheless these words of ours can serve to realize a specific purpose: They can be understood to express something that is not at all susceptible to expression in the language of "objective facts." (Huntington, p. 54)

In other words, the Buddha was a radical pragmatist: "What is true *(bhuta, taccha)* is that which bears results *(attha-samhita)*" (Kalupahana, p. 19).

I have tried to assume no knowledge whatever of Buddhism on the part of the reader, and no particular knowledge of literary theory, beyond that there is such a thing. Readers are cautioned, however, to jettison as much as possible of what they think they know about Buddhism, for instance that it is fundamentally pessimistic. "Life is suffering" is one of the Four Noble Truths, but life is also Nirvana. Life is suffering only because we misunderstand it. The same life can be paradise. Zen temples would not have such beautiful gardens, and Buddhism would not have produced such stunning artwork over thousands of years, if asceticism and pessimism were the whole story, or even very much of it. In fact, Buddhism is one of the most "optimistic" religions

around. It asserts that in every being there is the possibility of enlightenment, and in everything that seems ugly there is beauty. In everything that seems temporal, there is timelessness. But of course we can
only begin to go beyond suffering when we stop denying it. Buddhist
Enlightenment is not like being "saved" or "born again" in the Christian sense. It is a matter of opening the mind, clearing away blind faith,
and thinking clearly. There is no god in Buddhism, but it nevertheless *is*
a religion. This is a sticking point for many Westerners, from Catholics
and Jews who understand it to mean that they can keep their old religion and be Buddhists too, to nihilist/atheists and even pundits like
Andy Rooney for whom a godless religion is a *non sequitur*. Many practicing Western Buddhists get this wrong, or only partly right. One may
insist, for instance, that all the many Buddhist deities are simply representations of various aspects of mind, and not "real" at all, but without
realizing that the same is true of ourselves, of the one who makes this
observation.

I am very far from wishing to suggest, like most proponents of a
"religious" approach to literature, that all literature is, or ought to be, a
kind of scripture. Literature is just literature. It does not refer, after the
example of medieval allegory, to the life of Christ, or the lives of Mo-
hammed or Buddha, nor have any "salvational" aspect, nor should it.
To suggest otherwise is to embark on something quite different from
reading or literary study. We must not forget that "'Because enlightenment has no forms or formlessness' . . . 'sentient beings' and 'Buddha'
both vanish" (Cleary, *Entry into the Inconceivable*, p. 103).

There have recently been several books and many articles ad-
dressing affinities that may exist between Western deconstruction and
Buddhist thought. All of them are very different in scope and purpose
from this book. Harold Coward's *Derrida and Indian Philosophy* is an ex-
cellent, careful, and thorough examination of Derrida's philosophy of
language as compared to those of various classical Indian thinkers, including the Buddhist Nagarjuna. Coward takes great care to note differences as well as similarities, and he avoids unwarranted generaliza-
tions. His book is a good antidote to some other work that seems to
overlook important differences in the service of dubious ends.

Robert Magliola (*Derrida on the Mend*), for instance, has made an
interesting case for the similarity between Jacques Derrida's work and
that of the Buddhist thinker Nagarjuna. In particular, Magliola argues, I
think correctly, that Nagarjuna's concept of *shunyata* or emptiness is

very close to Derrida's *différance*. I am troubled, however, by his key assertion that Nagarjuna's thought "completes" Derrida's: "Nagarjuna's Middle Path," he writes, "the Way of the Between, tracks the Derridean trace, and goes 'beyond Derrida' in that it frequents the 'unheard-of-thought,' and also, 'with one and the same stroke,' allows the reinstatement of the logocentric too" (p. 87). To my mind, this belittles both Derrida and Nagarjuna, whose systems of thought are quite mutually exclusive in their means, origins, and ends, though similar in many specific and general aspects. Neither "needs" the other as Magliola would have it; and in fact his desire, as he admits, is to use Buddhism, a completely nontheistic system, to stake out a possibility of logocentric *theism* (Christian Catholicism) within Derridean *différance*—in other words, to place not only Buddhism, but deconstruction, in the service of Catholic Christianity.[2] (Magliola belongs to the Carmelite order.) This is a project worthy of an enlightened missionary, perhaps, but it is still decidedly colonialist, Western, and logocentric in its motivation and purpose. Relying often on categories of understanding derived from Derrida (logocentric or entitive, and differential), Magliola's readings of Buddhist thinkers are directed toward "improving" deconstruction for Christian and Catholic purposes. "I have been trying to show," he writes for instance, "that the Buddhist 'doctrine of the two truths' . . . permits the reinstatement of entitative theories while continuing deconstruction" (1990, p. 87). Derridean deconstruction itself already very explicitly allows for this possibility, though not in the definitive sense that Magliola intends; it has no need of the two truths to do so. What it does not allow, however, is theocentric logocentrism (Christian monotheism) as the terminus of differential thought, and in my opinion neither does Nagarjuna nor Buddhism in general. Putting the two together does not alter this fact. In the same essay, Magliola says that "My message to Westerners is that [Derridean] 'trace' . . . can be blissful . . ." (p. 96). But did anyone ever suggest that it could not be? Certainly not Derrida himself, or any of his followers in America that I am aware of.[3] Deconstruction is not a procedure that may be used or eschewed; it is a phenomenon in which all forms of knowing are subsumed, and logocentrism is one of its aspects. So are all forms of pleasure, including bliss.

Magliola and many others, moreover, ignore Nagarjuna's warning, cited previously, that "whoever makes a philosophical view out of 'emptiness' is indeed lost." As Coward puts it, "Language for Derrida is able to participate in that spiritual goal to which it points, but does not seem to do so for Nagarjuna" (p. 145). This fails to address the extremely important question of whether there is any place in a genuine Buddhist practice for literature, for reading, or for scholarship (much less philosophy), and the corollary question, of whether it makes any sense to address Buddhism from within these disciplines—is there any valid place for Buddhism in literature? Over and over again, many of the greatest figures in the history of Buddhism have sternly repeated Nagarjuna's advice against treating the Middle Way as "philosophy" or "literature," and it would be irresponsible in my view not to take those warnings seriously. I have found the same solution to this problem as David Loy,[4] though not by the same path, or to the same purpose:

> The end of views such as "ultimate" and "conventional" leaves the world as it really is—a *sunyata* or nondual world in which there is no linguistic or philosophical meddling. . . . Loy comments, "If there is no subject-object separation between language and object, between signifier and signified, then all phenomena, including words, are *tathata*, 'thusness.' This is why, as we see clearly in the Zen tradition, language too participates in the reality it manifests . . . [otherwise] how could so many Zen dialogues have led to a realization on the part of the student?" (Personal correspondence, quoted in Coward, p. 145)

There are important differences between deconstruction (and all forms of Western thought), on the one hand, and Buddhism, on the other, which the initial, perhaps overenthusiastic comparative approaches have tended to gloss over. I hope to respect those differences here, and to suggest, in a more practical and modest sense, what, if any, might be a way of reading and writing, of thinking literature, consistent with the principles of Buddhist thought. For if Buddhism does not let us know texts in ways that they cannot be known otherwise, students and scholars of literature, and philosophy too, might spend their time more profitably elsewhere. However, my purpose here is much more ambitious than Magliola's, as well as diametrically opposed to it: rather than yoking Buddhist thought to deconstruction and organized Christianity, I would like to find in the former ways of reading that allow us to dispense with both of the latter.

I have, not surprisingly, concluded that the closest thing in Western culture to the Middle Way of Buddhism is not any sort of theory or philosophy, but the practice of literature—reading and writing. The greatest potential in human being is its plasticity, its nonstatic, nonentitativeness, denied by all normative psychology, which defines change as exceptional, as occurring within a fundamentally static framework. Literature and Buddhism have in common that both recognize and embrace this plasticity. Another, corollary conclusion I have reached is that we should be wary of all attempts to mix Buddhist thought with Western theories, perhaps especially that of Derrida, since the latter is by Derrida's own admission so peculiarly and idiosyncratically Western. But my purpose is not to make a case (already made, to the extent that it can be, rightly or wrongly) for the "Buddhism" of deconstruction or the deconstruction of Buddhism, but rather to articulate ways in which Buddhism and literature might come together as *practice*, not theory. Buddhism has evolved, wherever it spread, in response to local traditions and needs. The ways of Buddhism in the Orient have always reflected that evolution. We cannot expect the specific forms of Japanese or Chinese or Tibetan Buddhism, which have been shaped over many centuries by highly idiosyncratic cultural settings, to respond to the needs of Western or particularly American Buddhists. I would like to think that this book represents one small step toward the establishment of authentic Western forms of Buddhist practice.

May everything be auspicious.

Part 1
(Anti-)Theory

1

Proust and the Bonsai Tree: Theories of Art Western and Eastern

East-West comparative studies must risk the charge of "Oriental-ism"—projection of positive or negative qualities onto a relatively un-known, "exotic" cultural other, to some latent or explicit ideological or political end—and this one is no exception. The purpose of any compar-ative study, of holding dissimilar things up to one another, is to allow an exchange to occur. It may be a good or a bad thing that such exchange cannot be entirely controlled, depending on one's point of view.

Several Asian religious traditions will be important to this discus-sion. It will be important to keep in mind that there are doctrinal differ-ences between Buddhism and Daoism, and Buddhism and Shinto, though the differences may be less important from a Western perspec-tive than the obvious affinities. The affinities—which explicitly pervade the art of bonsai—are perhaps best summed up for scholarship by Francois Jullien, who in several essays and books asserts the relative unimportance of mimesis in Chinese culture. The consequence is not only that there is no necessary barrier between speech and writing, or between reality and art or representation, but that writing, figuration (*wen*) is *natural*, not distinct from nature, and that "culture is the con-summation of nature. A "metaphysics of presence"—analogous to that which Derrida holds characteristic of Western logocentrism—pervades the entire system; yet the lack of any break or hierarchy between intui-tion, speech, and writing seems to undercut logocentrism" (Faure, p. 222). Though characteristic of several Eastern religions, this epistemo-logical view may reach full expression only in Buddhism.

Bonsai trees were first brought to Japan by Buddhist monks from China. The art of bonsai has been more shaped by the epistemology described by Jullien than any other, hence its privileged position in this discussion; bonsai has, moreover, reached its greatest degree of refinement in Japan, hence the prominence in this discussion of the latter country as exemplary of the East in general.

> When nothing subsists from an ancient past, after the death of beings, after the destruction of things, there remain alone, more frail but more tenacious, more immaterial, more persistant, more faithful, smell and taste, like souls, able to recall, to await, to hope, upon the ruin of all the rest, to bear without flinching, upon their almost impalpable droplet, the immense edifice of memory.
>
> —Proust
> *A la recherche du temps perdu*

> Sometimes a glance, a few casual words, fragments of a melody floating through the quiet air of a summer evening, a book that accidentally comes into our hands, a poem or a memory-laden fragrance, may bring about the impulse which changes and determines our whole life.
>
> —Llama Govinda
> *The Way of the White Clouds*

> A Sutra, as it is called, is all the ten quarters of the world. No time and place will be without its being a Sutra.
>
> —Dogen Zenji
> *Shobogenzo*

> Those who know what Nature does and know what humanity does have arrived. Those who know what Nature does live naturally. Those who know what humanity does use what their knowledge knows to nurture what their knowledge does not know. Living out their natural years, not dying prematurely along the way, they are rich in knowledge, but they still have a problem.
>
> That is the fact that knowledge depends on something to be accurate, and what it depends on is itself uncertain.
>
> —*The Essential Tao*

> Every day I attach less importance to intelligence.
>
> —Proust
> *A la recherche du temps perdu*

"That you should not be indifferent to religious speculations," a Japanese scholar once observed to me, "is quite natural; but it is equally natural that we should never trouble ourselves about them. The philosophy of

Buddhism has a profundity far exceeding that of your Western theology, and we have studied it. We have sounded the depths of speculation only to find that there are depths unfathomable below those depths; we have voyaged to the farthest limit that thought may sail, only to find that the horizon forever recedes. And you, you have remained for many thousand years as children playing in a stream, but ignorant of the sea. Only now have you reached its shore by another path than ours, and the vastness is for you a new wonder; and you would sail to Nowhere because you have seen the infinite over the sands of life."

—Lafcadio Hearn

The aesthetic of bonsai, the miniature trees cultivated for centuries in Japan and China, implicitly assumes much of what we aesthetic theorists in the West have only just figured out, having taken three centuries of laborious work in our mimetic art forms to arrive, past the point where representational art exhausts itself, at aesthetic possibilities that have been known in the East for millennia. Through the philosophy of deconstruction and recent developments in the theory of physics, the West has finally arrived at what the Japanese scholar above, quoted by Lafcadio Hearn, calls "the sea."

I am often asked by students what deconstruction is. My answer to the question is always this: deconstruction in practice is nothing more or less than asking stupid questions, if by "stupid" we can agree to mean questions that are not usually asked. The late Alan Watts, a lifelong student of Eastern religion and philosophy, resumed much of Zen Buddhism, as well as deconstruction, when he advised,

In thinking about human affairs, always call common sense into question. It is the most creative part of philosophy. Take ideas which are commonly accepted and which seem to be incontrovertible and question them. Turn them inside out and see what would happen if they were thought about in another way. (*Om: Creative Meditations*, p. 100)

In other words, deconstruction might be a way for "common-sensical" Westerners to conceptualize and contemplate "emptiness," the fundamental nonintegrity of the universe and of ourselves.—Nothing is entirely itself or anything else; subjectivity depends on and is contaminated

by objectivity and vice-versa; conventional truth (phenomena) and ultimate truth (noumena) are a nonintegrity that is not totalizable but not
contradictory either, or only apparently contradictory. A door can be,
and usually is, both open and shut—defined by the simultaneous possibilities of openness and shutness, which represent a continuum, not
an opposition. The reaction of "traditionalist" scholars to deconstruction is much like that of the uneasy disciples described by Watts in this
passage:

> A Buddhist scholar named Nogaguna, who lived about A.D. 200,
> invented a whole dialectic and founded a school where the
> "leader" of the students would simply destroy all their ideas—ab-
> solutely abolish their philosophic notions. And they would get
> the heebie-jeebies and see that the leader did not have the heebie-
> jeebies, that he seemed perfectly relaxed in having no particular
> point of view. "Teacher, how can you stand it? We have to have
> something to hold on to." And the teacher's response: "Who
> does? Who are you?" (p. 89)

Deconstruction may lead to the same questions.

What has bonsai to do with deconstruction or literature in general? Kyozo Murata, one of the great contemporary bonsai masters, has
defined the art form thus.

> Bonsai is a living plant transferred to a pot or tray or a rock or
> stone so that it can continue to live semi-permanently. It has not
> only a natural beauty of the particular plant but the appearance
> reminds people of something other than the plant itself. It could
> be a scene, a forest, or part of a forest, a lone tree in the field, a sea-
> scape, a lake, a river or a stream or pond. It is also possible that a
> certain appearance reminds a person of the wind blowing
> through the branches.[1]

This simple description points out several ways in which Japanese art,
including bonsai, is different in its means and its ends from that of the
West. The difference hinges on this: to "remind," as Kyozo Murata says
above, is not the same as to *represent*.[2] Where Western art embraces imitation of nature as something essentially other—assuming the alienation
of man from nature, the Japanese artist, imbued with the teachings of

Buddhism and native Japanese Shinto—similar to Native American forms of nature-worship—begins by assuming man and his art as indistinguishable from nature, and seeks to achieve not a copy of the natural world by artifical means (words or paint), but an experience of oneness with nature. In the case of bonsai, this is achieved through the medium of nature itself, living plants. A perhaps unfairly hyperbolic, though instructive idea of the practical aesthetic consequences of this difference might be obtained by a comparison of our Joyce Kilmer's famous poem, "Trees," with the following poem by the fourteenth-century Japanese Zen priest, garden designer, and poet, Muso Soseki (*Sun at Midnight*):

> The sounds of the stream
>> splash out
>>> the Buddha's sermon
> Don't say
>> that the deepest meaning
>>> comes only from one's mouth
> Day and night
>> eighty thousand poems
>>> arise one after the other
> and in fact
>> not a single word
>>> has ever been spoken (p. 110)

First, the experience of bonsai described above (to remind a person of "the wind blowing through the branches") is very close to Proustian involuntary memory, something that is *essentially ineffable*. Kyuzo Murata calls this bonsai concept of the sublime *wabi* or *sabi*, an aesthetic term associated with *cha-no-yu*, the tea ceremony, as elaborated by the sixteenth-century tea master, Sen no Rikyu. "From the verb *wabu*, to languish, and the adjective *wabishi* (lonely, comfortless)," *wabi* is closely associated with the severe aeshetic of Zen Buddhism (*Encyclopedia of Japan*, p. 1677). This poem by Fujiwara no Sadaie (1162–1241) "has been cited as suggesting the essence of *wabi*":

> As I look afar
> I see neither cherry blossoms
> Nor tinted leaves;
> Only a modest hut on the coast
> In the dusk of autumn nightfall.

Wabi originally meant simply "finding satisfaction in poverty," but within the context of Sen No Rikyu's style of tea, it has come to mean far more.[3] The *wabi* aesthetic grows quite naturally out of the Buddhist concept of emptiness, or the absence of inherent existence in phenomena. The synonymic concept of *sabi* refers to an aesthetic sense that results from the realization of Buddhist "emptiness": "A person awakened to the essential mutability of life does not dread physical waning or loneliness; rather, he or she accepts these facts with quiet resignation and even finds in them a source of enjoyment" (*Encyclopedia of Japan*, p. 1289). This might equally describe the aesthetic askesis that overtakes the narrator Marcel at the end of Proust's *A la recherche du temps perdu*.

> The Noh play or ballet expresses its movement in a relatively short period of time; on the other hand, you can hardly notice the slow growth of bonsai. The object of bonsai is to simulate nature. Nature expresses eternity in very, very slow movement and bonsai demonstrates this concept of the slow process of nature. When your concept of bonsai comes this far, then you cannot avoid going into the world of Wabi or Sabi. It is an almost impossible task to try to explain the meaning of these terms because they are concepts of feeling which were created and actually only felt by Japanese people over many, many generations; they were unknown to Westerners until recently.
>
> Wabi is a state of mind, or a place, or environment in tea ceremony, or in Haiku. It is a feeling of great simplicity, quiet yet dignified. Sabi is a feeling of simplicity and quietness which comes from something that is old and used over and over again. For an instant, picture yourself standing at a corner of Ryoanji's stone garden in Kyoto in the evening, in late autumn in a misty rain. You are viewing the garden; the next moment you close your eyes and are deep in thought. Actually there is nothing in your mind. It is empty, and yet your mind or heart is fulfilled with certain contentment. That feeling is Wabi.
>
> I firmly believe the final goal of creating bonsai is to create this feeling of Wabi, or Sabi in bonsai. This is the ultimate goal of the art of bonsai. I do not have the knowledge to explain the essence of Wabi, or Sabi, but I cannot help but think that the essence of philosophy is to seek truth, virtue, and beauty, and it so happens that these are the essence of bonsai.

The feeling of Wabi, or Sabi, is something almost stoic which eventually leads us to Zen Buddhism. These are not easy-going feelings; they are very disciplined, quiet but severe. The feelings are common among people who are very religious and people who create bonsai. I think this feeling is love, love for trees, love for human beings (Kyozu Murata).

The art of bonsai seeks, then, to achieve a wordless state of spatial and temporal transcendence *within the ordinariness of space and time*—a kind of *transcendence through immanence*, achieving askesis by immersion in the everyday.

Traditional classics of Japanese prose narrative such as Lady Murasaki's *The Tale of Genji* or the eighteenth-century *Ugetsu monogatari* by Ueda Akinari reflect a similar sense of artistic purpose. Like Western prose fiction, their content includes much of daily life, in the court or the countryside, but the style is far from that of the Western realist novel. The Japanese narratives are allusive, erudite, ambiguous, lyrical, and elliptical all at the same time.

A curious mosaic is the result, rich in rhetorical devices from earlier prose and poetry. The formal cadence of Chinese classics, pillow-words from early Japanese poetry, and expressions that echo [earlier works such as] *The Tale of Genji* . . . achieve the desired combination of lyric and narrative qualities. . . . Ordinary images and obscure literary allusions both serve to intensify the mood, the former by adding intimacy and familiarity, the latter by suggesting depth and profundity. . . . Acrostics, logograms, puzzles, riddles, and all manner of play on words have long been popular in Japan.

At times the cadence breaks into song, in a union of poetry and music. . . . Like a *noh* play or a Gregorian chant, the flow of sound rises and falls in a solemn yet lyrical melody, because the texture of the language more nearly resembles that of traditional drama or poetry than that of modern prose fiction. (Leon Zolbrod, Introduction to *Ugetsu monogatari*, pp. 60–61)

At all times and in all ways, classical Japanese narrative strives to *suggest*, rather than state.

By contrast, Proust, as an exemplary practitioner of late modern Western realism, deploys the resources of representational art to achieve their own exhaustion, to lead us to the point where involuntary memory, transcendental immanent experience, or, in Buddhist terms, the realization of emptiness, occurs *outside the boundaries of the text*. Juxtapose what Kyuzo Murata says above with the following passages, one from Proust, in which the experience of involuntary memory is explicitly discussed, and one from Maurice Blanchot's commentary on the Proustian sublime:

> That being who was reborn in me when, with such a shudder of happiness, I heard that noise common to both the spoon touching the dish and the hammer striking the wheel, to the unevenness of step of the flagstones in the Guermantes courtyard and of the baptistery of Saint Mark's, etc., that being is nourished only by the essences of things, in them only does it find its sustenance, its delight. It languishes in the observation of the present where the senses cannot bring it this essence, in the consideration of a past which the intelligence dries up, in the anticipation of a future which the will constructs out of fragments of the present and past from which it has withdrawn still more of their reality, retaining of them only that which serves the utilitarian and narrowly human end which it assigns them. But if a noise, an odor, heard or smelled before, should happen to be heard or smelled again, at once in the present and in the past, real without being contemporaneous, ideal without being abstract, then the permanent and habitually hidden essence of things is liberated, and our true self which, sometimes for very long, had seemed dead but was not entirely, awakens, stirs itself, receiving the celestial nourishment which is brought to it. One minute free from the order of time has re-created in us, by the perception of it, the man liberated from the order of time. And we understand this man's confidence in his joy, even if the mere taste of a madeleine cake does not logically appear to contain the reasons for that joy, we understand that the word "dead" has no meaning for him; situated outside of time, what can he fear from the future? (*A la recherche du temps perdu*, vol. III, pp. 872–73; my translation)

> To live the abolition of time, to live this moment, rapid as "lightning," by which two instants, infinitely separated, come (little by little, though all at once), to meet each other, uniting like two presences which, by the metamorphosis of desire, would identify each

other and themselves, this is to traverse all the reality of time, and in traversing it to feel time as space and empty place, that is to say free from events which always ordinarily fill it. Pure time without event, moving vacancy, agitated distance, interior space in process of becoming, in which the ecstasies of time dispose themselves in a fascinating simultaneity, what is all that, after all? What but the time of story, time which is not *outside* time but experienced as *outside* it in the form of a space, that imaginary space where art finds and disposes its resources. (Maurice Blanchot, *Le Livre à venir*, p. 23, my translation)

To create and sustain that space, that sense of emptiness or "the inherent unreality of things," has long been the goal of the Asian arts, and it is nowhere more acutely present than in the fully realized bonsai. This is too often misconstrued as a kind of nihilism. *Wabi* or *sabi* and the Proustian sublime, or experience of temporal transcendence, are two sides of one point,—facing in opposite directions.

I wish to consider Proust as an exemplary case, characteristic of all high modern, and to an even greater extent, "postmodern" Western art forms: the traditional representational means of art are forced to betray themselves, revealing the negative outline of what cannot be represented, what is in effect the antithesis of representational specificity— whether in words, paint, or marble—and of linear thought and experience. A successful bonsai would deliberately induce the kind of temporal and sensual *slippage* that characterizes what Jacques Derrida has called *différance*. For Westerners, this is the "death" of representational art—as Mallarmé, one of the great prophets of Western postmodernism, put it, "la fin du livre et le commencement de l'écriture," "the end of the book and the beginning of writing"—the endpoint of Western attempts to compete with nature, to arrive at a copy *better than the original*, an effort that might be said to have begun with the use of shadow and perspective to achieve a "photographic" quality on canvas during the early European Renaissance. This effort entails a hubristic, competitive stance with regard to the natural universe; hence the prominence in Western culture of such legends as Prometheus, the fire-stealer, recast by Mary Shelley in her "Modern Prometheus," *Frankenstein*; and Sisyphus, who is condemned to forever roll the same stone up the same hill, never reaching the end of his labor, a story firmly embraced by the twentieth-century stoical philosophy called existentialism. Transgressing the limits of the natural world has constituted the essence of heroism and at the same time the basis of our most profound anxieties, in our arts since the late Middle Ages, and in every other realm of knowledge since Descartes proclaimed humankind's fundamental difference from nature and superiority to it in the name of the Christian God, in his *Discourse on Method*, in 1637.

The Japanese have not generally sought to "compete" in this way with the natural—until they began to be influenced by the West. In sharp contrast with most Judeo-Christian and Islamic teachings, the Japanese traditional religion, Shinto, as well as Buddhism, affirms that not only humans, but animals, trees, mountains, and even stones are infused in varying degrees with *kami*, or spirit, and the Shinto conception of this world as an essential part of the gods' realm, not irremediably tainted by sin or evil, has deeply affected Japanese Buddhism.[4] So rather than seek to transgress on nature in the name of improving on it, assuming alienation while proving man's dominion over the natural, Japanese "artifice" embraces the natural, starting from the premise of oneness with it, to the end of repeating the most intense moments of human experience in nature ("the wind blowing," with all the affective associations that may accompany an individual experience of the wind in trees). The difference is subtle, like the difference between reminding and representing. Subtle, and difficult to express (to represent) in words because it occurs at the very limits of what words (or paint) can accomplish.

The Japanese attitude toward nature can seem perplexingly contradictory to Westerners. What are we to make of a people whose culture on the one hand expresses its sense of oneness with nature in so many ways, from the traditional architecture of its dwellings to such highly evolved art forms as bonsai, while on the other hand pushes whale species to the brink of extinction?[5] But this is not so paradoxical as it may appear. Western environmentalism shares with the exploitative capitalism it decries a view of human beings as fundamentally different from nature, their differences having to do with what comes next: protection, or exploitation for profit. Environmentalism in general proposes to protect nature not by asserting a greater human intimacy with it, but by *increasing* the barriers, legal, real, and metaphysical, between humans and nature so that the latter is protected through isolation from all things human. Extinction is often seen as preferable to captive breeding of endangered species because human interference compromises the "wildness" of animals.

In Japanese culture, there are countless legends and myths in which animals turn into people and back again, in which humans actually marry animals that have assumed human form, and in which animals are familiars, or messengers of benevolent deities.

> All kinds of animals are taken care of in the temples of some [Japanese] gods: stags, pigeons, herons, ravens, tortoises, carp, foxes, which are taken for a kind of God-like messenger. These animals are not worshipped as the ibis, the crocodile, the ichneumon, the cat and the steer were worshipped by the Egyptians. (Albert Brockhaus, *Netsukes*, p. 135)

At first glance, this may appear quite like the animals of Aesop or La Bruyère, but the difference is great. For Aesop and La Bruyère, and most other Western fabulists, and in modern animated cartoons—even the best ones—the physiognomy of animals is a disguise for human characters and actions, an encoded depiction of human, not animal behavior. If real animal behavior plays any role, it is as metaphor for human (see for instance Richard Adams's rabbit epic, *Watership Down*).

Japanese animal representations, however, often depict the animal as a fellow creature with its own unique traits, whose behavior has no certain implications for humanity's. It might be said that the usual Western fabulist tendency is turned on its head by the Japanese: instead of animals representing human characteristics, Japanese folklore often has animals per se assuming human form, but retaining all their specifically animal perquisites and behaviors. Foxes (disguised as humans) are said to have been the lovers and even the wives of men, all the while remaining tragically true to their fox nature. In the most fanciful superstitions, foxes, badgers, and other animals are assumed to freely interact with humans, but not necessarily or probably in a manner subject to human control or understanding. They are forces of nature, as inescapable and unpredictable as any other, to be reckoned with on more or less equal terms, and in any event not to be condescended to. This letter, for instance, is from the archives of the Todaiji, a Buddhist temple at Nara; it is addressed to the Fox God, a spirit of nature, by the famous Shogun Hideyoshi.

Kyoto, the seventeenth day of the Third Month

TO INARI DAIMYOJIN:—

My Lord,—I have the honor to inform you that one of the foxes under your jurisdiction has bewitched one of my servants, causing her and others a great deal of trouble. I have to request that you will make minute inquiries into the matter, and endeavor to find out the reason of your subject misbehaving in this way, and let me know the result.

If it turns out that the fox has no adequate reason to give for his behavior, you are to arrest and punish him at once. If you hesitate to take action in this matter, I shall issue orders for the destruction of every fox in the land.

Any other particulars that you may wish to be informed of in reference to what has occurred, you can learn from the high-priest YOSHIDA.

Apologizing for the imperfections of this letter, I have the honor to be

> Your obedient servant,
> HIDEYOSHI TAIKO

(reprinted in Hearn, *Glimpses, of Unfamiliar Japan*, pp. 319–20)

The traditional, unwesternized Japanese finds it difficult to comprehend animal protectionism because he or she does not think of him- or herself as exploiting nature, but rather as participating in the natural cycles and forces of nature, according to which there is no difference between a man killing a whale for food and a hawk dispatching its prey or a shark devouring a seal. As Takao Suzuki writes,

> This difference between the Western *Weltanschauung* and ours is, in a word, a contrast between the idea of discontinuity [with nature] and that of continuity. The former standpoint makes man's superiority [to animals] absolute, whereas the latter makes it only relative. (p. 104)

There is evidence that the modern Japanese relation to nature has been influenced by the Euro-West. In the late nineteenth century, not long after Japan had been reopened to commerce with the world, Lafcadio Hearn wrote that the

> fearlessness of wild creatures is one of the most charming impressions of travel in these remoter parts of Japan, yet unvisited by tourists with shotguns. The early European and American hunters in Japan seem to have found no difficulty and felt no compunction

in exterminating what they considered "game" over whole districts, destroying life merely for the wanton pleasure of destruction. Their example is being imitated now by "Young Japan," and the destruction of bird life is only imperfectly checked by game laws. (*Glimpses*, p. 612)

Western religious concerns would appear to have been active in seeking to change the Japanese mind on this point:

In one of the Yokohama papers, there appeared a letter from some holy person announcing, as a triumph of Christian sentiment, that a "converted" fisherman had been persuaded by foreign proselytizers to kill a turtle, which his Buddhist comrades had vainly begged him to spare. (p. 613)

One may well wonder how much of what we blame (or admire) in the Japanese—like their indiscriminate kiling of whales—they learned from us (or vice versa). It is, for instance, undeniably true that in Japan, particularly, Western realism, in the form of the novel, has been embraced by the literary culture and has profoundly affected the native forms of prose narrative, just as Chinese literary styles and forms did in earlier ages. Thus the works of the twentieth-century novelist Eiji Yoshikawa, for instance (*Taiko* and *Musashi* being the best known to Westerners) are in form as much like the novels of Tolstoy or Balzac as anything being written in the West now, and quite unlike older, traditional Japanese narratives.

Nonetheless, despite exceptions, differences remain, not only in the realm of nature, but of language and art—beginning with the fact that these are not as separate in Japanese thought as in ours. The Japanese begins with an assumption opposite to our own regarding language, assuming that it is an expression of his or her embeddedness in the natural world, not an arbitrary system of signs. The bat is thought of as a sign of good fortune, not evil, because the character for bat in Chinese is homonymic with the character for happiness. Similarly, the pine tree is considered a symbol of unrequited love because the word for pine, *matsu*, is a homonym of the verb "to wait." Japanese culture is permeated by such "fallacious" homonymies, which intricately weave together human language, thought, and civilization with the natural world. If such modes of thinking are fallacious, they may be less so than our own, according to which language is arbitrary and "unnatural," pure human artifice. It cannot be so if language itself, as the most recent research in animal communication suggests, is a fundamentally natural phenomenon, the means by which all higher animals bind themselves to and interact with the world they inhabit.

' On this point deconstruction and the arts of the East must part company. Where deconstruction begins with the premise that all representation is "empty," characterized by "absence," the Buddhist or Shinto priest might say that this is only true of "secular" art, which cannot really be art at all. This reveals a trap in which Western art of all genres was bound to be caught, a trap set in motion by the assumption of humanity's qualitative difference from nature. Deconstruction is merely the logical development of that premise, which it shares with mainstream Western science and religion (Judaism, Christianity, and Islam), and which engulfs sacred no less than secular art in ungrounded signifiers, Derridean *différance*. While the Buddhist asserts that all material forms are empty and unreal "when considered as separate independent entities," he or she believes also that they are "real in essence since they all emanate from the same Buddha nature" (*White Lotus*, p. 118).

In practical terms, this means that there are only two grand possibilities for art. One is Derridean/Saussurean "absence," which leads to our artistic culture of the "special effect," of pure artifice; the other is one in which the only real art must be "religious"[6] in nature, and characterized by an essential presence, binding the languages and modes of expression of humans, no less than those of animals, to nature and the cosmos. This is reflected in certain ceremonial practices. Among Tibetan Buddhists, for instance,

> when a work of religious art is finished it is generally brought to a *bla ma* for consecration (*rab gnas*). During this ritual, which is often quite complex, the wisdom being (*ye shes pa*) that corresponds to the deity in the work is invited to enter the work in order to become one with it (*gnyis su med pa*). From this point on, the figure is said to contain the living presence of the divinity. Being in the presence of a consecrated image is considered equivalent to being before the enlightened being itself. Although the tradition realizes that this awareness may be impossible for ordinary beings to achieve, it maintains that those who have attained the level of spiritual accomplishment called the "Samadhi of the Stream of the Doctrine" can see paintings and statues as if they were the deities themselves. That is why, in the Tibetan tradition, works of

art are treated with veneration, and why they are placed on altars and worshipped with offerings. (*White Lotus*, p. 138)

This is not "primitive" fetishism; on the contrary, it goes with a rigorous and systematic skepticism.

Buddha did not want people to follow him blindly, but rather to do so using their intelligence. He unambiguously stated: "O Bhik-shus and wise men! Just as a goldsmith examines well his gold through burning, cutting and rubbing it, so should you accept my word. But do not accept it merely out of respect for me." The objective study of the facts, as important in Buddhism as in science, is a striking parallel between them. . . .

[Buddhism] involves the philosophy of "dependent arising," an approach essentially in harmony with modern scientific methodology. Dependent arising (reliance upon causes and conditions) touches upon everything in the Buddhist world. Were Buddhism based merely on faith, it would not be able to face the challenge of scientific scrutiny. Scientists and Buddhists are working closely together these days and contributing much to each other. (*White Lotus*, pp. 98–99)

We might say then that the Buddha was advocating deconstruction, as I defined it. But this does not explain how a sense of *presence* in art could arise from skepticism.

To begin to understand this, however, we need look no farther than the growing skepticism of Western science with respect to some of its most basic assumptions about matter and our knowledge of it. The physician and philosopher Israel Rosenfield has documented this change particularly as it relates to our physiological and philosophical concept of consciousness. We cannot, argues Rosenfield, understand human consciousness solely by reference to the physical properties of the brain, no matter how sophisticated or exhaustive our understanding of the latter.

One might imagine reproducing brain functions in a computer, but it is an open question if one could build a sufficiently dynamic "computer body" to which its perceptual mechanisms could refer to enable meaning and understanding to emerge. Part of the extraordinary adaptibility of living things derives from the complexity of the bodies by reference to which their brains create understanding of the world. If we isolate a brain, no matter how sophisticated our techniques, we can never understand its function, because a brain does not function independently of the body it exists in. A brain in a jar is not a brain at all; we can learn some limited things from it, but we must recognize the limitations of that knowledge. (*The Strange, Familiar, and Forgotten*, p. 139)

Compare this statement by a contemporary Western medical doctor to the following one by a teacher of Tibetan Buddhism:

The fact that we say 'my body' and 'my mind' shows that neither of these two is the 'I.' Because neither the body nor the mind is the 'I,' therefore the collection of body and mind is not the 'I.' We should resolve that the reason why the 'I' cannot be found within the body or mind is because it is merely imputed by conceptual thought. It is because of this that the 'I' totally lacks any form of inherent existence. (*Buddhism in the Tibetan Tradition*, p. 118)

Similar arguments against the idea of a purely mechanistic universe evolved through random selection are becoming more prevalent among theoretical physicists such as Roger Penrose.

It is hard for me to believe, as some have tried to maintain, that such SUPERB theories [as the Theory of Relativity] could have arisen merely by some random natural selection of ideas leaving only the good ones as survivors. The good ones are simply much too good to be the survivors of ideas that have arisen in some random way. There must, instead, be some deep underlying reason for the accord between mathematics and physics, i.e. between Plato's world and the physical world. (*The Emperor's New Mind*, p. 430)[7]

The notion of a universe comprising only phenomena is no more false to a Mahayana Buddhist, however, than one comprising only noumena or spiritual essence. The truth is both conventional (phenomenal) and ultimate (noumenal, or *empty*). We can only begin to conceive the nature of "self" if we admit its nonintegrity, as both Rosenfield and the doctrine of emptiness assert. Mathematics, a "science" that is at once entirely imaginary and yet capable of predicting precisely the outcome

of physical phenomena, provides a conceptual basis for the noncontra-
diction of these two, which, according to Esoteric or Tantric Buddhism,
only appear to be mutually exclusive.

The limitations of mechanistic science, alluded to above by Rosenfield, can be appreciated within the realm of art by juxtaposing Japanese (or Chinese, for that matter) paintings or prints with traditional
Western postmedieval paintings. We in the West, since the Renaissance
and continuing into the present, have cultivated a taste for trompe
l'oeil—literally, "eye tricking." This is the basis of our representationalist painting. The very notions of shadow, light, and perspective, as articulated and practiced by the Renaissance masters, is trompe l'oeil, a
form of static special F/X. In this context, everything, from the physical
brain to language and artistic expression, become "special effects," the
results of complex but mechanistic artifice. The ultimate special effect is
alluded to by Rosenfield in the passage above: the creation of artificial
intelligence or consciousness. More primitively, there are famous exam-
ples of popular Renaissance "eye-trickery" that go beyond the framed
canvas: the entire interior walls of some villas in Italy were painted in a
manner to make the walls "disappear," giving way to vast, looming
architectural fantasies: balconies, columns, stairways, peopled by fro-
zen, apparently three-dimensional images of the lord, lady, children,
and servants of the household, and beyond these, distant landscapes,
looking almost more real than those outside. These enormous and intricate "indoor outdoors" are precursors of the modern cinema, with its
array of F/X that delight by the same paradox as the Renaissance villas
and paintings, the paradox of artifice so ingenious and intricate, so perfectly executed, that it seems "natural." We have arrived at a point in
our culture where perfect representations of the real are no longer even
of much interest; instead, we are most drawn to playful, "baroque" (in
the original meaning of the Portuguese barroco: weird, strange) deploy-
ments of technical wizardry in ways that call into question the very nature of reality as our representationalist culture has conceived it. We are
on the verge of full realization of the "virtual reality" imagined—pre-
dicted—over a hundred years ago by Joris-Karl Huysmans in the decadent manifesto, *Against the Grain*.

The bonsai master may already be where we are just arriving.
He got there from the other side; his way has not entailed the laborious exhaustion of mimeticism. Japanese literature did not need Flaubert, Proust, or Joyce to wring realism's neck, never needed a Picasso,
Matisse, or Rodin to turn perspective inside out, did not need a Max

Ernst to turn the means of realism to surreal ends, has had no need of Derrida's playful obscurantism or Mallarmé's beautiful, sterile poetry. Japanese poetry, painting, sculpture, and the other art forms not recognized as such by our culture, such as garden-design or bonsai, have changed very little over the past thousand years.

Early on, the East eschewed attempts to "simulate" three dimensions within two, to try to "compete" with nature through artifice. Instead, Chinese and Japanese painting and printmaking concentrated on an elliptical, restrained, almost enigmatic use of form and color, influenced by the elaborate calligraphy of Chinese and Japanese writing. Rather than attempt to "duplicate" natural scenes, an endeavor that must sooner or later admit its futility, the Chinese and Japanese have sought to depict certain highly specific yet abstract aspects of nature— "the wind blowing in the trees," what Kyuzo Murata refers to above as *sabi*. This "mathematical" (precise yet abstract) aesthetic is apparent in the silk paintings hanging in Chinese restaurants, as well as in museums; see for instance the famous prints of Katsushika Hokusai or any example of *sumi-e*, Japanese ink painting. This art frankly admits and embraces itself as art; it makes no effort to duplicate or compete with the real by deploying a battery of special effects such as perspective, or light and shadow. Even when perspective is a factor in Japanese art, as in some of the woodblock prints of Hiroshige, it exerts a geometric force within two dimensions, rather than attempting to sustain the illusion of three. Even with some deference to formal perspective, Eastern landscapes typically collapse three dimensions into two, not abolishing the distance between trees in the foreground and Mount Fuji in the back, but ignoring it. Not because they could not do otherwise, not because the concepts of light, shadow, and perspective are unknown to the artists or beyond their technical skill (as in American folk art, whose charm may have something in common with Eastern aestheticism) but because they elect not to, in the service of a self-conscious effect. Kyuzo Murata puts it this way:

> In a Japanese Kabuki play, a male actor plays the role of a female. We call him Oyama. The audience knows that she is he, but he really acts and looks like a woman. This is an art. The same can be said about the art of bonsai.

The art is highly aware of itself as art, highly stylized. The closest Western conceptual equivalents might be formal poetry and the opera. Instead of

attempting to deploy every possible artifice in order to abolish its difference from the real, this sort of art begins by accepting the difference,
and embracing it. This way, it loses its difference from the natural real
and becomes one with it. By contrast, our mimeticism finds fault with
any novel, play, or even poem in which characters do not sound like
"real people."

In the nineteenth-century, following the end of the Edo period
(1603–1868) and the Tokugawa shogunate which had sealed Japan off
from intercourse with foreign cultures, this very different aesthetic
began to interest Western painters like Paul Jacoulet, grown weary of
realism.[8] Without an infusion of Eastern aestheticism, our arts might
have evolved quite differently. Proust himself associates one of his most
important metaphors for involuntary memory with the Japanese:

> And just as in that game in which the Japanese amuse themselves
> by dropping into a porcelain bowl filled with water small bits of
> paper previously shapeless but which, scarcely plunged into the
> water, unfurl, take on shapes and colors, each one becoming dis
> tinct from the others, turning into flowers, houses, consistent and
> recognizable characters; in the same way now, all the flowers of
> our garden and those of Monsieur Swann's park, and the water
> lilies of the Vivonne, and the good people of the village and their
> little houses and the church and all of Combray and its environs,
> all that took on form and substance, emerged, the town and its
> gardens, from my cup of tea. (*A la recherche du temps perdu*, I, p. 47)

The association may be coincidence—happy for my purposes here—or
it may be something else.

Either way, it points to the most important aspect of bonsai, which
makes it an epitome of Japanese and Eastern art, the medium itself: living plant material. Nature is embraced not only conceptually, but physically. The natural process of plant growth and development becomes
completely fused with, indistinguishable from the artistic expression.
No artist, however great, ever achieves mastery of his medium, never
perfectly controls it. The Eastern artist, and in spite of himself, by a
more tortuous path, the Western artist as well, must not just accept, but
embrace the impossibility of autonomy or control, and enter into complicity with contingency, with the slippage innate to any medium,
words, paint, or stone, and the slippery evanescence of "meaning." Only
by doing so can he or she achieve the sense of presence that Buddhism

ascribes to art. This presence is not the symptom of a nostalgia for total-ization or logocentrism, but the insight that all dualities of observing subject and observed object are illusory, that all such apparent forms are void, but that everything is nonetheless present to itself.

At the beginning of this chapter, I cited a passage from the Dao. That passage continues as follows:

> Real people of ancient times did not know to like life and hate death. They came to life without rejoicing and went to death with-out resisting; they simply came unencumbered and went unen-cumbered. They did not forget their beginnings or look for their end. They accepted their lot gladly, then returned to it without minding.
>
> This is called not diminishing the Way by the mind, not try-ing to help the divine by means of the human. Such are called real people. Those who are thus have a focused mind, a quiet counte-nance, and a relaxed brow. They are as cool as autumn, warm as spring; their emotions correspond to the four seasons. They have expedients for dealing with people, and none know their limit. (*The Essential Tao*, p. 105)

In the West, it has required the heavy flourishes of deconstruction to lead us to the same conclusion: that the essence of art is in such slippage, in the impossibility of control by artist or observer. Form and meaning are always virtual, never static and never complete. This implicitly as-sumes something that all our Western museums are in business to deny: no art is forever. No cultural artifact, however magnificent or ad-mired, is immortal. When a bonsai tree dies, as it eventually must, it is no longer art. Though the tree may live for a thousand years, the bon-sai master accepts the eventual mortality of his work, and in so doing he may come to terms with his own. A similar attitude is reflected in the way in which every Japanese shrine is routinely rebuilt at regular intervals—on the same site, by the same methods, in an architecturally identical manner, with exactly the same materials, but rebuilt nonethe-less, or perhaps "duplicated" would be a better way of putting it, its lease of temporal existence "renewed." The form is the same, but part of the essence of the sacred place is this perpetual renewal, reflecting the cyclical repetitions of nature.[9] The Chinese concept of immortality assumes the same relativism; the mythological sages or "immortals," said to have discovered the "elixir of immortality" and transcended the limits of ordinary physical existence by entering a perfect state of immanence, of identification with nature, were understood to prolong their material existences, not indefinitely, but for a few hundred or thousand years only. In a similar way, "permanence" is something the bonsai artist strives to achieve, but in a *relative* sense, not an *eternal* one, thus in a rather different way from a Western painter, sculptor, writer, or even architect. The Zen priest and the bonsai master believe that only by embracing the natural cycle of life and death, growth and decay, can there be any intimation of eternity. Proust wrote, "How should I fear death, when I have died so many times before," while Confucious, about 2,500 years previously, said something quite similar: "As long as you do not know life, how can you know death?" (*The Essential Confucious*, p. 21).[10] In Buddhism, the "Buddha body cannot be attained without death, . . . without many deaths and resurrections. . . . The unexcelled yoga is a yoga of dying and resurrecting" (Thurman 1988, p. 124). The bonsai master thus accepts without question the limitations imposed by working on a living medium, not merely assuming but celebrating that the goal of art, for artist or beholder, is neither the finished product in or for itself, nor the art object, per se, but to induce a sense of *wabi*, of oneness with temporal nature and its vicissitudes.

> In the art of bonsai, there is no particular school for teaching technique as you have in flower arrangement. This is because we must protect the life of a tree permanently. Limiting the bonsai technique to a certain style is to ignore the physiology of the tree. If you try to enforce your own particular design on the tree without considering its nature, the tree may eventually die. . . .
>
> All of you who are actually engaged in the art of bonsai have at one time or another studied under fine bonsai teachers and have mastered the techniques of Chokkan or upright style, Moyogi or octopus style, Shakan or slanting style, and Kengai or cascade style, but when it comes to Nebari—arranging root systems or branches—you realize that it does not always work as it is taught.

Thus a bonsai is never finished, never complete. A bonsai masterpiece cannot be hung on the wall or set on a pedastal and left alone. It must be continually tended, fed, watered, trimmed. As old branches die back, new ones grow. The connoisseur of bonsai must also be an artist, for the object is always in progress, never static, unless it dies, when it is no longer bonsai at all. Buddhism has a similar view of other religious art forms: artists "are trained in art conservation and restoration, since it is the practice in temples and monasteries to keep statues and paintings as close to their original condition as possible to fulfill their religious function" (*White Lotus*, p. 128). The notion of aesthetic closure is simply irrelevant. There can be no such thing as a "definitive edition," a "perfect restoration" of a bonsai tree, just as recent theorists have suggested that there can be no definitively closed, completed works of literary or plastic art. These objects exist within a culture defined by mutability. Shakespeare's plays are a different sort of experience today than they were for his contemporaries. Peter Greenaway's textually faithful film enactment of *The Tempest*, *Prospero's Books*, would be incomprehensible to the bard himself, or any patron of the Globe Theater. What may have been in the seventeenth century quite close to spoken vernacular sounds to us today like a strange verbal chamber music, richly evocative but having almost no relation to the language we speak. In fact, our literary and artistic monuments are quite like trees, always requiring cultivation. This is why criticism, academic and popular, is necessary. The critic tends the masterpieces handed down within the culture, pruning here, growing out a leaf or a branch there. This is not to say that every critic does the job equally well.

As far as the literal life of the medium, there is nothing comparable in Western art to bonsai, except perhaps contemporary performance art, in which the living body of the artist him- or herself is the medium of expression. Performance art is a recent development in Western history, and an outgrowth of reactions such as surrealism against realist traditions, assumptions, and rules.

To the mind steeped in Western modes of art, bonsai might appear nothing more than a different instance of representationalism. The goal of bonsai, however, is not to copy trees as they are in nature, but rather to arrive at a living embodiment *of our idea of a tree*. Francois Jullien has elaborated the way in which mimesis is replaced in Chinese art and literature by a sense of the *wen* (mark, sign) as *déploiement*, unfurling, an outgrowth of nature. Culture is a development of nature; so is art; there is no division betwen artifice and nature, so that there is no such thing as artifice in the Western sense. The Chinese tradition—which was absorbed intact by the Japanese—is opposite to the Saussurean idea of the arbitrary nature of the sign. The Daoist Lu Xie expressed this by saying "The reason why words can arouse the world is that they are the *wen* ('patterns') of the Dao" (quoted in Faure, 201). Or more explicitly: "Man is the jewel of the Five Phases;/He is the spirit of Heaven and Earth;/The spirit manifests itself and language is founded,/Language is founded and then *wen* appears./This whole process is perfectly natural" (quoted in Faure, p. 221). Marcel Granet sums this all up in *La Pensée chinoise* by saying that Chinese words are *emblems* rather than signs (Granet, p. 42). The seventeenth-century Chinese *literati* painter Dong Qichang elaborates:

> Painters of the past usually took the old masters as their models, but it is preferable to take Heaven and Earth [i.e., nature] as teachers. One should observe every morning the changing effects of the clouds, break off the practising after painted mountains and go out for a stroll among the real mountains. When one sees strange trees, one should grasp them from the four sides. The trees have a left side, which does not enter in the picture, and a right side which does enter, and it is the same way with the front and back. One should observe them thoroughly and transmit the spirit naturally, and for this purpose the form is necessary. The form, the heart and the hand must correspond mutually, and one must forget all about the imagination [what the spirit offers]. Then there will, indeed, be trees in the picture, which have life also on the silk; they will be luxuriant without being crowded, vigorous and elegant without blocking the view, all fitting together like members of one family. (Chu-Tsing Li, "The Artistic Theories of the Literati," p. 20)

Kyuzo Murata elaborates the same concept for bonsai:

> There was a famous Zelkova which was owned by the late Prime Minister Shigura Yoshida, who happened to be Chairman of Nippon Bonsai Association at the time. This bonsai was created by Mr. Ogata. He had severed the main trunk of the zelkova and created a totally new look. When I first saw it at the annual Kokufukai Exhibition, I laughed, and so did the directors of national museums who attended the exhibition. Several years later it was again exhibited at the Tokyo Olympics and people liked it this time. Some years later it was displayed at another Kokufukai Exhibition, and this time it was recognized as one of the finest bonsai in Japan. It really is a strange looking tree. You would never find

such an unnatural-looking tree anywhere in the world, yet it looks exactly like a huge zelkova tree standing alone and strong in the field.

Or like our *idea* of such a tree. This means that the art of bonsai aims (1) to perfectly unite theory with practice—something that recurs throughout Eastern thinking—so that every fully realized bonsai is at once its own theory and *exemplum*, and (2) to perfectly fuse human imagination with natural process—or to perfectly reflect such nondistinction, if we admit that it already exists. Dong Qichang expressed the idea in the following manner.

> The Dao of painting is to hold the whole universe in your hand [if you possess the real spirit of art, you can comprehend everything]. There will be nothing before your eyes which is not replete with life, and therefore painters [who have attained this] often become very old. But those who paint in a very fine or detailed manner [*kehua*] make themselves servants of Nature and impair their longevity, because such a manner adds nothing to the power of life. (Chu-Tsing Li, p. 20)

Another way of putting this would be to say that the true works of art, painting, bonsai, or whatever, become powerful channels of what is called in Chinese *chi*, or life force.[11] The French scholar Rolf Stein has written in a classic work on the subject that

> a certain mana (*ling* in Chinese, *linh* in Sino-Vietnamese), a vague but beneficent magical power, is inherent in miniature gardens. . . . like all magical powers, this quality is not only negative, averting evil; it is also positive. It brings strength and power. An elderly Japanese man named Takamuro, who lived around 1764–80 (the Meiwa and An'ei reign periods), retained despite his old age a "shining" skin (that is, not dried out), a feature of a young man. When asked where he got this vitality, he replied that, as a youth, he had cultivated *bonsai* . . . and that with the support of his imaginative thought . . . he had not aged. (pp. 49–50)

In Japanese, and in Shinto, the place of *chi* is replaced by *nagare*, meaning "flow," the essence of natural being, characterized by mutability. To induce *chi* or *nagare*, other names for the mysterious and paradoxical presence alluded to in all Buddhist theories of art, to enter his or her work, the artist must first become a channeler of it him- or herself. Before nature can be imparted to the work, the artist must achieve personal naturalness. For in the Eastern context, if that naturalness does not exist, in us or in our art, the fault must lie in the human, not in nature. Contrast this with the implicit goal of almost all realist (including the "naturalism" of Zola and his followers) and symbolist Western art, which begins by accepting the mutual alienation of human and natural: to make a surrogate reality out of human thought that is so well realized as to make us forget our alienation from what is before and around us. So great a poet and art critic as Baudelaire thought anything natural to be evil and an aesthetic abomination. Western abstract formalism, while eschewing the referentiality of earlier art, displays a similar rejection of the natural: all meaning must arise from "pure" form and color, which bears no relation to any real or natural object. In this way, "modern" Western art carries on the ideology of realism. This premise subtends most mainstream Western art, philosophy, and religion—Judaism, Christianity and Islam—in most of their forms, and while it has produced much of extraordinary beauty, that beauty conceals a fundamental disjuncture, a sense of loss, a wound that may only be irremediable within the premises of Western thought. That aspect of Western art *as a work of mourning for some unspecified loss* has interested me as something apparently common to all forms of art and philosophy in the West.[12] Until I had looked at Asian traditions, I could not figure why our arts in the West should have this in common. I assumed that it must be an inevitable characteristic of human expression. Proust manages to escape these limitations of his art only by the most elaborate and costly, in personal and aesthetic terms, even cumbersome artistic apparati, becoming a bedridden, neurasthenic invalid, confined to a cork-lined room by necessity, not choice. James Joyce completed a similar metaphysical journey from within Western traditions, but it led him to a similar dead end, the hermetic narcissism of *Finnegan's Wake*. That scholars exist who consider this his greatest work is a reflection of what is wrong at the heart of Western aesthetics, metaphysics, and daily life. That breach is the reason why we are a massive proliferation of contradiction, why Jacques Derrida has been able to say that America, the most grand, successful, and hyperbolic material expression of Western thought, *is différance*. Buddhism asserts that this sense of loss, of absence, of a never-ending work of mourning, as I have called it elsewhere, is preliminary to the final stage of enlightenment, which must bring an apprehension of occulted presence in and around us. Enlightenment, in Buddhist terms, consists in a careful *deconstruction* of the self through contemplative study and meditation. The self, and its corollary, the subject/object binarism foundational to Cartesian metaphysics, is understood by Buddhist epistemology as illusion.

> [The student or novice] must experience the sensation that we might have if, instead of having the eyes and the brain in the head, we had them in the hand and then the hand was able to examine the head and the body, reversing the normal process which is to look downwards in order to see the hands or the body. . . .

> One attains, by means of these strange drills, psychic states entirely different from those habitual to us. They cause us to pass beyond the fictitious limits which we assign to the *self*. The result being that we grow to realize that the *self* is compound, impermanent; and that the self, *as self*, does not exist. (David-Neel, *Magic and Mystery in Tibet*, p. 277)

Not only is this true of the self as we conceive it, but according to Buddhist teaching, even "Gods, demons, the whole universe, are but a mirage which exists in the mind, 'springs from it, and sinks into it'" (David-Neel, p. 287). However, our Western traditions of linear rationalism, or logocentrism (which goes back much further than Descartes, and even than Aquinas) leaves us at a cul-de-sac, with no way of rediscovering presence except by renouncing Cartesian skepticism and burying our intelligence—an act of self-mutilation—in fundamentalism, blind faith, or cult. We wonder that these two things—Cartesian scientism and zealous bigotry—can be so prominent in our Western culture at the same time. Yet they are two faces of one thing.

Proust's style is characterized by the tendency to aphoristic paradox. In my reading and experience, the closest that Western thought, or deconstruction, ever comes to reaching beyond its limitations has been in this kind of style: some of the work of Franz Kafka, for instance (particularly *The Great Wall of China*), and in criticism, the work of the late Paul de Man: "We do not see what we love, but we love in the hope of confirming the illusion that we are indeed seeing anything at all" (1986, p. 53). Here is another of de Man's "maxims": "The hour of truth, like the hour of death, never arrives on time, since what we call time is precisely truth's inability to coincide with itself" (1979, p. 78).

Such formulations not only pervade de Man's writings but are the core of them.

The genre they most resemble is the Zen Buddhist *koan*. A *koan* is a "problem" in words, a logically irresolvable paradox—an aporia, in our Western literary terms—devised by Zen masters "to stop their students' word-drunkenness and mind-wandering." But a *koan* need not be a written text at all.

> Each person grasps spiritual enlightenment through different *koan*, and in most cases some accident works as a *koan*. . . . When a *Zen* master called Kyogen-Shikan (?A.D. 898) was sweeping a garden, a small stone happened to hit one of the bamboo trees, making a sound. He experienced spiritual enlightenment by hearing it. In other words, *kyakuchiku* (hitting the bamboo tree) worked as a *koan* for him, or he actualized it as a *koan*. . . . All the phenomenal things of the world before us are *koan* because we are able to actualize them as *koan* and because this fact has been proven by the various actions of the most eminent *Zen* masters of the past. (Takahashi, p. 15)

There have been many reports of bonsai being actualized as *koan*, and this makes sense: nowhere else is human attention so concentrated on the essential voidness *(shunyata)* of nature, and on the essential nondistinction *(pratitya-samutpada,* dependent arising) of human mind and artifice from nature. As for textual *koan*—and this is admittedly a factitious distinction—in addition to being statements that appear to erase, or undo themselves, they are riddles, or questions, to which "There are many right answers and there are also none" *(Zen Flesh, Zen Bones*, pp. 11–12). *"Controlled or not controlled?/The same dice shows two faces./Not controlled or controlled,/Both are a grievous error"* *(Zen Flesh*, p. 119). "The doctrine of the T'san [Zen] sect," wrote Alexandra David-Neel, "has been defined by one of its followers as 'the art of perceiving the polar star in the Austral hemisphere'" (p. 278).

All of this may begin to suggest why the arts and humanities have been increasingly marginalized in the West, at least since the early Renaissance and Descartes: if we accept the two fundamental premises of mainstream Judeo-Christianity and Cartesian scientism—our difference and superiority with respect to nature, and our consequent moral freedom, even obligation to subjugate and exploit all its aspects—then art can only serve as the acolyte of Science, for Science, in Descartes' vision, is the instrument of our dominion over, and alienation from the natural world. Those who study art, scholars in the humanities, are relegated to a double inferiority, as acolytes to acolytes. By accepting this role, we have been complicit, as artists and humanists, in our own irrelevance to our larger culture. More important, we have abdicated the greatest responsibility of the arts and those who study them: to affirm the place of humanity in nature.

2

Reading Emptiness:
Proust with Nagarjuna and Dogen Zenji

This chapter pursues the same issues in the same comparative vein as the last one, but in a more academic and literary context. It was conceived in answer to a graduate student's question. All of her teachers, she said, read works of literature in quite different ways, according to different theories or methods, including the antitheory theory, according to which all theories are bad; most of these theories led to contradictory, even mutually exclusive results when applied to the same text. One professor gleefully embraced every theory, applying each, willy-nilly, to the poor poem until his students reeled in dizzy confusion. Where then, she asked, was the *truth* of the literary text? Must not only one of these readings really be the best one? How to tell which? And what about the text itself? How can it have any value unless there is only one correct reading of it?

The problem for the graduate student in literature, or any careful reader, is analogous to that resolved in Buddhism by the "Middle Way," or *Madhyamika* system of thought, founded by the great Indian Buddhist philosopher, Nagarjuna.[1] Nagarjuna is said to have expressed the problem in a famous maxim: "Regarding the same female body, an ascetic, a lover, and a wild dog entertain three different notions: 'A corpse!' 'A mistress!' 'A tasty morsel!'" (*Master of Wisdom*, p. 39). But Buddhist thought has not often been considered by students and scholars of literature, partly because of the pervasive idea that textuality implies a kind of mediation inimical to the "direct experience" that Buddhist practice seeks to achieve, and also because of the traditional disciplinary boundaries, according to which Buddhism is the exclusive province of a small community of specialists in religious studies. In this chapter I hope to show that Buddhist thought does not proscribe textuality, that in fact reading, writing, and even literary theory in the West can be consistent with the principles of Buddhist practice. Buddhist thought may even provide Western literary theory with what the graduate student (to whose question I began by alluding) found missing from her education: insight into the nature of literary truth.

The Middle Way as conceived by the *Prasangika* or "Middle Way Consequence School" embraces two apparently contradictory truths, that of dependent arising *(pratitya-samutpada)* and emptiness *(shunyata)*. Emptiness is identical with *dharmakaya*, or ultimate reality; the ultimate reality is the lack of inherent existence in any thing, person, or thought. But this does not deny the existence of things as phenomena, on the level of phenomena.

> 'Exists' is the dogma of eternalism. 'Exists not' is the dogma of annihilation. [But] You [the Buddha] have revealed the Dharma [of dependent co-origination], free from the two extremes. . . .
>
> [That which] has transcended the duality of being and non-being, without however having transcended anything at all; that which is not knowledge or knowable, not existent or non-existent, not one or many, not both or neither; [that which is] without foundation, unmanifest, inconceivable, incomparable; that which arises not, disappears not, is not to be annihilated, and is not permanent—that is [reality], like space, not within the range of words or knowledge.
>
> Just that is dependent co-origination; just that is what You maintain to be *sunyata*. The true principle (saddharma) is of that kind, and the Tathagata [the Buddha in his *nirmanakaya* aspect, as "intermediary between the essential and the phenomenal world"] is like that also. It is also accepted as the truth, the ultimate meaning, suchness and the real. It is the indisputable. Whoever awakens to this is called Buddha. (Nagarjuna, pp. 19, 25)

According to the "Exposition of Bodhicitta," "[The three natures]—the imagined, the dependent, and the absolute—have only one nature of their own: sunyata [*shunyata*]. They are the imaginations of mind" (p. 43). Emptiness itself is no exception: it is critically important to understanding emptiness that "Even the abstraction through which sunyata is conceived You [the Buddha] have declared non-existent." *The Philosophy of the Middle Way* asserts that "The Victorious Ones have announced that emptiness is the relinquishing of all views" (*Philosophy of the Middle Way*, p. 223).

To know emptiness as identical with dependent arising is to realize enlightenment. "The taints of apprehending the two truths as different entities are what make it impossible for anyone but a Buddha to perceive directly both phenomena and their final nature, emptiness, at the same time" (Sopa, p. 316). Removing those "taints" is the work of all Mahayana and Vajrayana Buddhist practice. As the Heart Sutra, the core scripture of Zen Buddhism, says, "all five *skandhas*"—the five sensual and mental continuums, of phenomenal form, sensation, perception, mental reaction, and consciousness, that comprise the self—"are empty."

> . . . form is no other than emptiness,
>   emptiness no other than form;
> form is exactly emptiness, emptiness exactly form;
> sensation, perception, formulation,
>   consciousness are also like this.
> . . . all things are essentially empty—not born, not destroyed;
> not stained, not pure; without loss, without gain.
> Therefore in emptiness there is no form, no sensation, perception,
>   formulation, consciousness;
> no eye, ear, nose, tongue, body, mind,
> no color, sound, scent, taste, touch, thought;
> no seeing and so on to no thinking;
> no ignorance and also no ending of ignorance,
> and so on to no old age and death and also no ending of old age and
>   death;
> no anguish, cause of anguish, cessation, path;
> no wisdom and no attainment. Since there is nothing to attain,
> the Bodhisattva lives by Prajna Paramita,
> with no hindrance in the mind; no hindrance and therefore no fear;
> far beyond delusive thinking, right here is Nirvana . . .
>
> (Aitkin, pp. 173–35)

Implicit in the teaching is that even the concept of the *skandhas* is not to be taken too seriously.

> "Repository [consciousness] exists"; "The person exists"; "Only the psychophysical aggregates exist"; "Only the bases of consciousness exist": Teachings such as these are given out of

consideration for those who do not understand the more profound meaning [of teachings about emptiness].

Even though the Buddha held no philosophical view of a
real, substantial self, nevertheless he used the expressions "I" and
"mine" while teaching. Similarly, even though entities are devoid
of intrinsic being, still he taught in a nondefinitive sense *(neyartha)*
that they all do exist. (Chandrakirti, p. 162)

This implies that "The purpose of the Buddha's teachings about the
skandhas, elements, and so forth is [merely] to dispel the belief in a
self. By establishing [themselves] in pure consciousness the greatly
blessed [Bodhisattvas] abandon that as well" *(Master of Wisdom*, p. 41).
The dualism of samsara—of the suffering world of phenomena, the literary world of signs, and of *shunyata* and Nirvana, or the absolute
truth of literature (or anything else)—is like all dualisms untenable
within emptiness, so that *nirvana is right here*, it is the same as this world
of phenomena, all around us, if we can only recognize the essential
emptiness, nonintegrity, of forms, including words.

Zen is typically thought to denigrate words and texts in favor of
direct experience, but the great Japanese Zen master "Dogen himself
argues that words are valuable, *not because of their capacity to represent reality (mimesis) but because of their power to produce it.*" Words, texts, are instances of dependent arising, "metonymies" of *shunyata*, bodhi mind,
just as are all phenomena. Dogen wrote in *Tenzo-kyokun* that

The monastics of future generations will be able to come to understand a nondiscriminative Zen *(ichimizen)* based on words and letters, if they devote efforts to spritual practice *by seeing the universe
through words and letters, and words and letters through the universe.*
(Quoted in Kim, p. 95; my emphasis)

An essential corollary of emptiness is that "Truth has no essence; it exists only through its effects and in particular through speech."(Faure, p.
241). This can only be true so long as we remember that phenomena are
devoid of inherent existence. Forms, whether texts or extratextual expe-
riences, seem independently real because of our tendency to reification,
to grasp at what we perceive.

The perceiving mind is equally void. "All our knowledge," wrote

Lafcadio Hearn in a statement derived from the Japanese expressions of
Mahayana, "is derived and developed, directly or indirectly, from
physical sensation,—from touch."

> Of course this is no ultimate explanation, because nobody can tell
> us *what feels the touch.* "Everything physical," well said Schopen-
> hauer, "is at the same time metaphysical." But science fully jus-
> tifies the Buddhist position that what we call Self is a bundle of
> sensations, emotions, sentiments, ideas, memories, all relating to
> the *physical* experiences of the race and the individual and that
> our wish for immortality is a wish for the eternity of this merely
> sensuous and selfish consciousness. (Hearn, "Nirvana," *Gleanings
> in Buddha-Fields,* pp. 226–27)

Hearn was right; science still does confirm this view of consciousness
as something that cannot be meaningfully separated from sensuous experience, and yet cannot be reduced to it either. Israel Rosenfield, physician and philosopher, has written that

> a sense of consciousness comes precisely from the *flow* of percep-
> tions, from the relations among them (both spatial and temporal),
> from the dynamic but constant relation to them as governed by
> one unique personal perspective sustained throughout a con-
> scious life; this *dynamic* sense of consciousness eludes the neuro-
> scientists' analyses. (Rosenfield, p. 6)

This is what Franz Kafka meant when he wrote that "The decisive moment in human development is a continuous one" (p. 163). The self is a
work-in-progress. Nothing about it is definitive or irrevocable. We can
alter it by the smallest choices, of what to read, for instance, or what to
write. What if we were to consider reading and writing in such a light,
as parts of the ongoing construction—and deconstruction—of our own
consciousness, individual and collective? Perhaps that is what I wish to
propose, or to suggest has already been proposed, but not stated outright in the terms of contemporary literary theory.

   Essential to the realization of emptiness is that dependent arising—the swirling maelstrom/pageant of the world we experience—
does not exist independently of us and our perceptions; we are interde-
pendently related to all that we see around us, and to every text we

read. And interdependent origination is not to be understood as a simply temporal phenomenon; it is simultaneous and instantaneous as well as historical. That is, everything at any given moment exists in a relation of interdependence. Texts are like Zen gardens: what we see depends on what we bring to the seeing. This is not a nihilistic way of looking at things, but quite the opposite. All of nature becomes in this perspective a vast kaleidoscope held up to the eye of mind: thus it has been suggested by an Amerian Zen master that "human thought evolved as the taxonomical array of animals and plants, giving richness of metaphor to the human mind." On a more somber note, "When species die out, metaphors die with them and no longer inhabit the mind" (Aitken, p. 102). The toucan's gaudy bill, the wild colors of parrots, the shark's murderously pure economy of form, the strange, wonderful shapes and colors of every large and small animal, all are inseparable from our own mind, our own being, our own incredible capacity for thought and experience. This is why Zen master Bankei told his students, "When you become a Buddha"—which literally means, when you become *aware*—"there isn't any place to go. You're already everywhere" (p. 127).

To realize emptiness, and its principal corollary, dependent-arising —to really see and experience this aspect of reality directly—this is in all Mahayana Buddhist traditions to cut the root of karmic accumulations and samsaric experience. "When the single root of mind is cut, the leaves of samsara, such as dualistic clinging, perish" (Dowman, p. 84). "Once mortals see their nature, all attachments end" (*Zen Teachings of Bodhidharma*, p. 35).[2] To know emptiness is the goal of all Buddhist practice; in Zen and the Dzog-chen or "great perfection" yoga of Tibetan Buddhism, direct experience of *shunyata* is the culmination of all practice. As for Zen master Dogen, it does not lead to denial, but affirmation, of this world of phenomena, and of words; in literary study, it does not shatter the text, but illumines it. From the perspective of emptiness, every (re-)reading, every "theory" and antitheory is indispensable— and superfluous; as Proust put it, every one is "the angel who disappears as soon as he has opened the gates to the celestial garden."

The fact of emptiness is confirmed by modern physics. Nobel-prize-winning scientist Richard Feynman says that "there is nothing that living things do that cannot be understood from the point of view that they are made of atoms acting according to the laws of physics," and yet, what are atoms? They are nothing more, according to the scientists themselves, than mental constructs. "French physicist Bernard d'Espagnat maintains that atoms, as well as all other knowable entities are mere properties of nothing other than space or space-time" (Wallace, 42). Other post-Einsteinian physicists such as Stephen Hawking have elaborated on the purely subjective nature of "time": "Disorder increases with time because we measure time in the direction in which disorder increases," making the second law of thermodynamics, the law of entropy, "almost trivial" (Hawking, p. 147). And of pure space, the physicist John Gribbin has said that his discipline can tell us absolutely nothing. Everyone is by now aware of Heisenberg's uncertainty principle, according to which we cannot observe any phenomenon without affecting it; moreover, according to Gribbin,

> If we cannot say what a particle does when we are not looking at it, neither can we say if it exists when we are not looking at it, and it is reasonable to claim that nuclei and positrons did not exist prior to the twentieth century, because nobody before 1900 ever saw one. (Wallace, p. 43)

We can only perceive according to our sense organs, and there is no way to prove that what we perceive has any reality apart from our perceptions. The literary theorist Paul de Man was referring to this fact when he wrote that "we do not see what we love, but we love in the hope of confirming the illusion that we are indeed seeing anything at all" (p. 53). This is simply another way of saying what the Buddha said, that our desire is *grasping*: the wish to know that what we see is really there as we see it, *independently existing*, to conflate what we think we perceive with what is really there when we are not looking. Nonspecialists are used to thinking that the world described by scientists is quite real, but the scientists themselves often think differently.

The truth of dependent arising is the truth of phenomena, all of which are ephemeral and depend on an endlessly concatenated chain of prior causation, just as a word must signify only by resemblance to and difference from other words within a semantic field of signification, a language, or a specific text, a poem or story. The specific meaning of words is constantly evolving as the semantic field, the language itself, changes. According to the Middle Way, there is no essence anywhere in reality as we know it. There is emptiness, which is the lack of inherence, or essence; just as no word can mean without reference to other words, so the "I" which is me in the present must refer to everything I have said, done, or thought in the past, and to every aspect of me now or in the past—my hair, my toes, my fingernails, my sleeping and waking thoughts or "mind," none of which, by itself, is me. "I" cannot be said to have any inherent or positive existence because "I" as an integral totality cannot be demonstrated to exist. A great Tibetan secret text of *Dzog-chen* supposed to be by the yogi Padmasambhava says that

> . . . even though it is one, you cannot look for it in any particular
>   direction.
> It cannot be seen as an entity located somewhere, because it is not
>   created or made by anything.
> Nor can it be seen as just being empty, because there exists the
> transparent radiance of its own luminous clarity and
>   awareness. (Reynolds, p. 26)

There is no "I" apart from the simultaneously chaotic and orderly agglomeration of physical and mental pieces, past and present, which I am and have been in the past.

In just the same way a poem has no inherent essence; its meaning or essence can only be imputed, and this can be done in many different ways, according to many different "theories." Similarly, the self can be studied *as a phenomenon* in many different ways, physical, psychological, philosophical, and from many different and specialized perspectives within each. Even among medical practitioners, the individual self will be conceived very differently by, for instance, a podiatrist and a psychiatrist. Each correctly sees a certain *conventional* truth about the individual; but the fact that none of these parts adds up to an integral, essential whole that can be said to exist independently of its (infinitely divisible) parts is the higher truth of emptiness. The same can be said for any work of literature.

Essential to the "Middle-Way Consequence" or *Prasangika* system is that the absolute truth of emptiness can only be reached by working through the relative or conventional truths of phenomenal reality or "reading." The relative truth is not false, but the obverse of *shunyata*, its other face. Dualism is characteristic of all relative truth, but *shunyata* is absolutely nondual, so that all oppositions such as true/false, now/then, and present/absent are meaningless within it. Derridean or deconstructive theory is a supertheory of conventional, relative truths;

it attempts to account in theoretical terms for the lack of inherence in all theories, including itself. In literary practice, we are accustomed to thinking in terms of dualisms (signifier/signified, sign/referent, the process of signification, or *différance* within a text which gives rise to meaning, or the Derridean *trace*), but what would be the *shunyata* aspect of literature, the ultimate truth of emptiness that subsumes all relative truths? Elsewhere[3] I have described it by the term *gnosis*; it is what every literary text can only say by not saying, the "untext" within every text. What Proust said of dreams is true also of poems and novels: "[They] are not realizable, and we know it; we wouldn't have any if it weren't for desire, and it is useful to have them in order to see them fail"—or in order to see what they say without saying—"and so that their failure"—their 'saying without saying'—"may instruct" (Proust, III, p. 181).

If there is a dialectic of gnosis and apparent meaning in every properly literary text, then we must consider the Zen *koan* as a privileged instance of literariness. *Koan* in Japanese means "public announcement"; the corresponding Chinese term *kung-an* referred to a legal decision important enough to establish precedent for other cases. The *koan* in Zen practice is an apparently irresolvable paradox or aporia such as "What color is a flower you cannot see?" Many *koans* use logic to expose logic as a rhetorical convention, rather than as "truth"; many serve to radically destabilize our habitual belief in a reality that exists apart from our perceptions (How can we *be sure* that a falling tree makes noise unless *someone* hears it? How can we know that there are positrons if no one thinks them, or what atoms do when we are not looking?).

Until recently, most Western studies of the *koan* embraced the idea that Zen is an essentially antiword and anti-intellectual system of thought, in which enlightenment and textuality are mutually exclusive, and the *koan* has been thought of only as a verbal tool for breaking habitual patterns of thought that impede access to direct experience of the mind's emptiness. Yet, in the work of Bernard Faure and Steven Heine in the West, and the school of Critical Buddhism in Japan, which has re-read Japanese Buddhist traditions in the light of Tibetan sources, a very different attitude toward the *koan* and the word has been revealed in such Zen thinkers as Dogen. Thomas Kasulis writes that

Dogen is very much a part of the Zen tradition in recognizing that discursive language is not necessary for enlightenment, yet he also grants the value of verbal exposition. In fact, in the final analysis, [he] maintains that the two means of transmission are not at all separate, but are two dimensions of the same reality. (Kasulis 1985, p. 89)

For Dogen, the *koan* may not be textual at all—"a Zen Master called Reiun-Shigon . . . grasped the way at the sight of some peach blossoms in full bloom," so that he "actualized them as *koan*" (Takahashi, p. 15)—and there is no essential difference between a textual *koan* and a nontextual one. There is no reason to be surprised, for to insist on the mutual exclusivity of textuality and *satori* would be to fundamentally betray the *Madhyamika* system, according to which all dualisms, all apparent contradictions, are samsaric delusion; to insist that enlightenment can occur only in a state of extratextual ontological "purity" would reflect an *unenlightened* view of phenomena and emptiness, phenomena and mind, as separate things. According to the Tibetan *Dzog-chen* view, "Appearances are not erroneous in themselves, but because of your grasping at them, errors come into existence" (Reynolds, p. 25).

Dogen at least was not guilty of such error, though he appears to contradict himself on the question of literary pursuits. Most American Zen students are familiar with Dogen's admonishment in *Shobogenzo-zuimonki*, an introductory text, against "literature," even including Buddhist scripture: "People who study the way should not read the scriptures . . . These days, Zen monks"—including, he admits elsewhere, himself—"are fond of reading literature, composing poetry and writing dharma discourses. This is wrong" (*Shobogenzo-zuimonki*, p. 82). Perhaps this is advice that Dogen considered necessary for beginning students; certainly most Zen teachers since have given the same advice, but perhaps without fully understanding Dogen's reasons. As Isshu Miura said, repeating the thought of a Chinese Zen master, "Zen is 'without words, without explanation, without instruction, without knowledge.' Zen is self-awakening only. Yet if we want to communicate something about it to others, we are forced to fall back upon words" (Heine, p. 60). And this is the fundamental paradox of Zen, that it should denounce literature and art while contributing more to Japanese artistic culture than perhaps any other institution. But this should not surprise, for Zen, like the Middle Way, *is* paradox. Heine writes that "Dogen maintains, in contrast to an exclusive emphasis on the priority of silence, that language is a necessary and effective means of conveying the Dharma."

He reinterprets the term *katto* (literally "vines," but by implication "entanglements," "complications," or "word-tangles"), which is often understood as an illusion and therefore an impediment to enlightenment, to suggest a *self-entangling/disentangling vehicle* for expressing spiritual realization that is never free from the need to be expressed. "Generally, although all Buddhist sages in their training study how to cut off entanglements *(katto)* at their root, they do not study how to cut off entanglements by using entanglements. They do not realize that entanglements entangle entanglements. How little do they know what it is to transmit entanglements in terms of entanglements. How rarely do they realize that the transmission of the Dharma is itself an entanglement." (Heine, pp. 5–6)

And this would be true no matter how the transmission occurred, textually, orally, or otherwise. The question is not whether to engage in "entanglements" but how; the "literary sin" that Dogen admonishes against must be that of merely repeating the entanglements, becoming tangled up in them unwittingly. This would amount to "fetishizing" or reifying literature or art, allowing them to become objects worshiped only for themselves, as though they were inherently existing. Dogen's *koan* practice, as Heine shows, consists in turning traditional readings of *koans* on their heads, deconstructing the accepted readings in favor of quite opposite interpretations. This can only mean that for him, *koan* practice consists in the act of creative reading, of *misprision*, as Harold Bloom calls it. Truth is in the act, not the content, of reading. Heine concludes that, like Bloom, Dogen believes that the text (poem, in Bloom's usage) has meaning but that its meaning can only be expressed as another text (poem). This is a radical departure from the commonly held view of the *koan* among contemporary Zen practitioners as "a hammer to beat down the walls of dualistic mind." Yet, it seems far truer to the spirit of Zen than the notion that there should exist a *solution*, a *correct*—though nonlogical—"answer" (in Japanese, *wato*) to each koan. (Some *koans* are admitted to have more than one "correct" *wato*, but these are limited and, usually, very narrowly defined.) It would appear that, in Dogen's view, any solution would instantly become a *koan* of its own.

He seems to suggest that that the *koan* should be seen not as a psychological tool that brings one to a labyrinthine impasse based on the paradoxicality of speech and silence, but as a *discursive means of generating shifting, self-displacing (and thereby self-correcting) parallactical perspectives.* (Heine, p. 7)

Nothing could more accurately describe the study of literature as I conceive it here: the use of entanglements to entangle entanglements.

> A Zen master said, "Birth and death, coming and going, are the real human body."
>
> Another Zen master said, "Birth and death, coming and going, are the real body."
>
> A third Zen Master said, "Birth and death, coming and going, are the real human being."
>
> Yet another Zen master said, "Birth and death, coming and going, are the real true body of the Buddhas."
>
> Four masters can each express it in their own way. All of them have straight nostrils, and they said it all right; but that's not quite it. If you asked me, I would not agree. Birth and death, coming and going, are just birth and death, coming and going. (*Rational Zen*, p. 56)

For all of us who are attracted to literary study, there is something in the texts we love that is greater than the sum of any of their parts, no matter how many times or how many different ways we take them apart and put them back together again, and yet absent from every reading, every positive statement or theory; only *virtually* present in our experience—call it reading or performance—of the text, and yet evanescent, unfindable on any particular page or in any particular line or stanza, nowhere present except in the act, the instant, of reading. Dogen says we should stop looking for it—not stop reading, or writing, but stop looking for something that is nowhere but in the act of looking.

> Cease and desist, and you are like an ocean taking in a hundred rivers. When you get here, there is no grasping or rejection.
>
> Let go, and you are like a great tide riding on a high wind. When you come to this, there is inside and there is outside.
>
> Buddhas do not know it exists; housecats do know it exists: do not put the ineffable secret of Zen in your little heart. (*Rational Zen*, p. 60)

Cease and desist—Students, stop asking your teachers to tell you the

truth, for like authors, they can only, in Proust's words, give you desires. There is inside and there is outside—there is no need for deconstructing dualisms; they deconstruct themselves, if we only let them.
"You do not need to leave your room," said Kafka; the "world will
freely offer itself to you to be unmasked, it has no choice, it will roll in
ecstasy at your feet" (Kafka 184). Buddhas do not know emptiness because they are it; to *know* something we must engage in the subject/ob-
ject duality, as a cat does when it hunts a mouse. The ineffable secret of
Zen is everywhere in front of our noses; in the computer key I just
struck, but only the last one, and only for the instant in which I struck it.

> If one can utter a statement at which the limits of the uni-
> verse vanish, one is still talking about good and bad luck in a
> spring dream. If one can utter another statement that will open up
> an atom to bring forth a scripture, this is still putting makeup on a
> beauty.

> If one directly illumines the true awakening that is not a
> dream, then one will see that the universe is not large and an atom
> is not small.

> Since neither is real, on what can a statement be based?

> A clam in a well swallows the moon; the jade rabbit at the
> edge of the sky sleeps by itself in the clouds. (*Rational Zen*, p. 65)

According to the Madhyamika system, the truth is never essentially present, but it is evident as emptiness in all phenomena, including words. Marxist literary theorists might dismiss such a statement
out of hand, yet one must wonder if their ever-insufficient, ever-
renewed attempts to reduce literature to money and matter (which are
just as "empty" as stones and flowing water, or words) must not be
fueled by the same desire, ever unrequited, that the rest of us feel, to
trap that elusive essence not just in words but things, commodities, the
material analogue of a warm body, so that it can be definitively embraced. That desire is deluded, of course; it reflects the innate human
tendency to reify. The essence of the story or poem is nowhere but in
ourselves, in the very act of reading. "Truth is produced, not revealed,
in a dialogical encounter that brings to mind the 'authentic' games ana-
lyzed by Gadamer, in which, like in a game, something that transcends
each participant's will takes over and words 'reveal' to them what they

are thinking" (Faure, p. 149). Thus "hermeneutics"—the belief in a meaning, a signified, within each text—"remains a case of what in Chan [Zen] parlance one might call 'seeking the depths for what one has left behind in the shallows.'" The truth is in the details of the act; emptiness is form, form is emptiness. "One is reminded," Faure writes, "of Linji and many other Chan masters stressing that there is no Dharma to be found, nothing to understand or to obtain" (p. 147).

This implies that scholarship too must be essentially "performative," "more concerned with 'the content of its form.'"

> Not unlike recent trends in literary criticism, Chan writers (or locutors) achieved (or tried to achieve) a "freedom from the signifier." There ensued a kind of weightlessness, a feeling of elation conspicuous in some of the *Recorded Sayings* literature, although it eventually turned into its opposite with the ritualization of the genre. (Faure, pp. 149–50)

Faure is quick to add what Zen practitioners already know, that "this feeling has not yet had a chance to pervade Chan/Zen scholarship" (p. 150). Is "performative" scholarship necessarily "relativistic," as many of my colleagues, who are constative critics, believe? Not necessarily. The Middle Way affirms two truths, one ultimate (emptiness), the other conventional, and it asserts that they are two faces of one thing (emptiness), but "the identity of the relative with the absolute does not collapse the distinction" (Faure, pp. 150–51). Relativism or naturalism "loses the Middle Path." To affirm one face of truth at the expense of the other is not permissible, but the distinction between the two must be kept, not fudged, in order to lose it. It can only be kept by scholarly rigor, *attention to detail*. No matter how closely we read, we cannot keep from projecting ourselves, but at the same time, we cannot keep the text from projecting us. According to the Middle Way, nothing is relative except what is absolute and ultimate. And every mutable phenomenon is quite fixed and absolute in our scrutiny of it. The truth is that we do not know precisely what literature is, any more than consciousness; or that we can only say what it is *precisely* in a very particular case, a very particular instant, and in the form of another text, another literary "performance." The only meaning of a text is another text whose truth, though absolute, lasts only as long as it takes to say it. Rigor is not separable from beauty; it is an aesthetic, not an objective phenomenon. Physicists admit this; why should not literary people admit it?

•

I would like to argue that literature is a privileged ground for the realization of emptiness. This is true because in reading literature, there can be no doubt that one is not dealing with an objective reality. To the extent that we insist, to ourselves or in critical practice, that texts refer to specific material and objective truths, and do not admit the emptiness of these, we defeat this aspect of reading, and fall into reification. To the extent that we read texts as collections of signs that can take the shapes and assume the importance of realities when we read, we directly experience the nature of emptiness, just as we do in dreams. As we realize that texts exist as literature only in the moment of reading, in the same instant in which we come into being with them as readers, we gain a direct experience of the nature of mind according to the Middle Way: the mind is nowhere to be found, neither any one of its parts nor exactly their sum. As Israel Rosenfield puts it, "A brain in a jar is not a brain," meaning not a *mind*.

Proust's great novel might be viewed as a quintessential, typically *grasping* text, because it expresses the desire of reification as *nostalgia*, a "search for lost time." Yet it ends with the extinction of that desire, a great conflagration of temporal desire and of the desire for (lost) time. And its ending joins with its beginning, like a dragon swallowing its tail. Might we not, then treat it like a vast *koan*?

So much of what we call literature, modern and ancient, springs like *A la recherche du temps perdu* from the longing for something lost in time. The narrator of Proust's story finds memory in the taste of a madeleine cake and a cup of tea, and embarks on a quest to discover the nature of time. In the course of his search, he sees the toll of desire on others, how it exhausts them—as when Swann says, "To think I wasted years of my life, that I wanted to die, that I had my greatest love for a woman I didn't like, who was not even my type!" (Proust I, p. 382). The narrator finally realizes that the landscape before him, whether the past of Combray or the present streets of Paris, exists only in his mind, and that time is no different from space.

If I had not accompanied Albertine on her long round, my mind only wandered the more for it and, for having refused to taste that morning with my senses, I enjoyed in imagination all such mornings, past or possible . . . for the sharp air turned the necessary pages of itself, and I found everything indicated before me, so that I could follow it from my bed, the gospel of the day. (III, p. 26)

Places have no reality for us, he discovers, until they exist as vividly in our minds as they do before our eyes, until we have *made them over again in our imagination*. This suggests that we need not actually go to a place to *be* there. "Houses, roads, avenues, are as fleeting, alas, as the years" (I, p. 427). Proust's characters change so much in the course of time that they no longer recognize each other; his narrator realizes, through experience, that desire is very like reading: the mind and its object are intricately intertwined. In a final phenomenological conflagration, the narrator of the novel has a kind of *satori*, in which he sees that both time and substance are illusory, and indistinguishable from consciousness: "I felt dizzy to see beneath me, yet inside me, as if I were leagues high, so many years." This is why men and women "touch simultaneously, like giants plunged into the years, such distant ages, between which so many days have come to rest—in Time" (Proust III, pp. 1047–48). Not only are space and time one thing, but both are the stuff of consciousness ("There exists no external object apart from consciousness [*Master of Wisdom*, p. 41]); this can only be said outright after the narrator has spent three thousand pages looking for time, a love object, and a vocation, outside of himself, when they were in him already. All those things—space, time, love, and even writing itself—*consciousness*—are *a story*. There is nothing to look for, nothing to tell—*so tell that*, the narrator decides, in the only way possible; live it and write it as one thing. So the writing of *A la recherche du temps perdu* became Proust's life to a degree that no work ever had or perhaps would again for any writer or artist, and the line between author and narrator became irremediably blurred. The only way to tell the story was to become it, to disappear into the writing of it. And in the reading, if we read Proust the way he wanted us to, the intensity of the novel makes our real lives seem dull, and we discover just as Proust's narrator did that consciousness and reading, like consciousness and time, are one thing. *What is the sound of one mind remembering? A page turning with the noise of a thunderclap.*

There is much in Jacques Derrida's work that points directly to the fact of emptiness.[4]

The unheard-of difference between that which appears and appearance (between the 'world' and the 'lived') [—the difference,

that is, between our sensory perceptions and what it is or may be
that we are actually perceiving, or between the atom that we think
and the atom that we "see"—] is the basis of all other differences,
of all other traces, and *it is already a trace.* (Derrida, p. 95)

This is a difference that cannot be measured, or even proved, because
we can never really know if there is any reality independent of our perceptions which is why the difference is, as Derrida writes, *inouïe*:
unheard-of, strange, unknown. What Derrida calls the trace is nothing
other than interdependent origination. "The trace is in effect the absolute origin of sense in general. Which comes back to saying, again, that
there is no absolute origin of sense in general. The trace is the difference
that opens up appearance and signification" (Derrida, p. 95). However,
Derrida, and deconstruction generally, articulate these phenomena
within a traditional, dualistic, European philosophical discourse. It is
true that Derrida attempts to subvert the forms of continental philosophical tradition by elaborate punning and playful obfuscation. But he
remains within the Cartesian tradition, writing and speaking from the
Cartesian vantage point of *the subject who is supposed to know*: "le sujet
supposé savoir." Thus deconstruction cannot see dependent arising and
emptiness except as objective phenomena, and only then by maintaining
the absolute distinction between subject and object, and by exempting
the subject from the "objective" effects in question. The consequence is
a critical discourse that seems to valorize the writing/speaking subject
(the deconstructionist, Derrida or another) above any objective reality,
since the subject is the only apparently stable phenomenon remaining.
Of course, the subject cannot logically be exempted from the epistemological consequences of *différance*, and Derrida knows this perfectly
well; nevertheless, his remarkable insights, so close to those of Buddhist philosophy, cannot be stated within the Western philosophical
tradition without apparently retaining the subject/object dualism and
thereby engaging a fundamental contradiction. In the terms familiar to
Western philosophy, this is a logical development; *différance*, while it
contains within it the deconstruction of all subject/object dualisms,
must first be stated in the terms of that very dualism. Once having been
so stated, however, *différance* was bound to spread like a virus: either
the contradiction resolves itself by becoming recognized and admitted,
giving way to new contradictions, or new formulations of the old one,
until it exhausts itself, or it persists unacknowledged, in both cases in-
fecting every statement made by a "subject supposed to know" with

irremediable nondistinction from that which is supposed to be known. If emptiness is a fact, then stating something like *différance*, or restating emptiness and dependent arising within the context of Western literary study, fundamentally alters the "reality" being addressed, and that reality includes the subject making the statement, and by extension, subjectivity in general.

Does this suggest that the doctrine of the Middle Way is unnecessary, that it has nothing really essential to add to the way we read literature? If deconstruction has already launched the concepts of emptiness and dependent arising within the general tradition of post-Hegelian continental idealism, what do we need Buddhism for? It is just as reasonable to ask, if *shunyata*, Buddha nature, is in everything, why should we not just accept that? Why do we need to discuss it, since discussion just introduces more illusory mediation from the "ordinariness" we are trying to embrace? And after all, has not the same point already been made by Western existentialism? This recalls a question put to Zen master Bassui.

> Questioner: ". . . If there is no mind-nature outside of this, then rising, standing, moving, and being quiet, seeing, hearing, recollecting, and knowing are simply the natural activities of heaven. What is the need of seeing into one's own nature?"
>
> Bassui: "That is the heretical view of naturalism. If you do not clarify your Buddha nature, you will get caught by the illusory body, thinking it is real. Not even in your dreams would you then understand the principle of one's true nature being one with phenomenon." (p. 112)

What this means is that without "clarification," without learning to understand our own nature, we cannot go beyond an experiential equivalent of the mimetic fallacy: living everything as though it were "real," as though we were independent subjects, perceiving an "objective reality." No progress can be made until this illusion is broken.

Literature offers a privileged ground for doing so, inasmuch as in literature there can be no question of objective reality. Jaron Lanier, a computer scientist who is said to have invented the term "virtual reality," along with the interface gloves indispensable to practical VR, writes:

> The experience of virtual reality forces you to notice your own experience of consciousness. In the physical world there's a fuzzy

boundary between the hypothetical objective environment and your way of interpreting it, but in VR the world that is presented to you is entirely a human artifact. (Lanier, p. 112)

Certainly this is true, but VR has existed for far longer than computers, or even film, in the form of literary experience. In the phenomenon of reading, we have an opportunity to observe the mind engaged with a fictitious reality, and to see the way it enjoys being lulled or seduced into believing in the "truth" of this fictive world. In the instant of reading or writing, the consciousness and the text are *one thing*. For example,

> The *Shobogenzo* is Dogen himself, who by his esoteric act has created "the half which exists through intimacy." In a remarkable sense, the *Shobogenzo* is Dogen's own presence—a discursive account of his own self-knowledge as presence and also the intimate presence of Dogen himself, in oneness of body-mind *(shinjin ichinyo)*. To separate Dogen (the physical presence) from his ideas (his mental presence) is to deny that oneness. Conversely, I must bring my whole self, body and mind, to the text in order to create my own esoteric act, my own "half which exists through intimacy." The very act of interpretation, then, involves the whole person, the body-mind unified through intensity of focus and held *(ji)* together in the personal act *(gyo)*, the continuous practice *(gyoji)* inseparable from enlightenment. (Kasulis 1985, p. 91)

After the instant of such oneness, the text remains as a residue, to be recathected by other consciousnesses. The relation of reader to text is not merely a prosthetic one, for text and "self" become organically *nondistinct* in the act and the instant of reading or writing; the self and the text are genuinely expanded outward. Hence the multiplicity of every text: each, melding with a new reader, must produce an entirely new text, which however is the same as the text before it was ever read by anyone. This position is as far from objective New Criticism and structuralism as from reader-response criticism, which defend above all the sanctity of the subject as agent, and the text as object, in the act of reading. But it also embraces all of these, as cases in which phenomena without any objective reality have been described as static and real. Thus, the realities they describe are neither false nor ultimately true, but merely conventional. That is to say, within the context of relative, phenomenal existence, they have validity. In Dogen's view,

Each interpretation, though fragmentary and limited, nevertheless exerts itself totally in its Dharma position, fulfilling its own
possibilities and destiny without obstructing others and without
being obstructed by others, in absolute freedom [but not ran-
domly or only "relativistically"]. Hence, philosophical and religious unity of expressions and vines is not of entity but of activity—that mode of activity in which "unity" is not contemplated in
terms of any metaphysical principle but is, instead, acted out.
(Kim, pp. 94–95)

And the ultimate meaning of all theories, all interpretative activities, is
emptiness.

To generate a new text, which is the same as melding with one
already written, we need first to realize the mind's and the text's emptiness. To do this effectively, we must, as the great Tibetan teacher Pabongka Rinpoche put it, correctly identify "the object of refutation": the
(reified) self and, for my purposes, the (reified) text as well. He describes in detail how this is to be done. To realize the independent self
as an illusion, we first must see the illusion clearly and directly—we
must catch the self looking back at us.

This instinctive form of grasping at the 'I' is something we have
always had in our mind-streams, even when dreaming. As long as
we do not meet with certain circumstances we will not be clear on
how the 'I' appears to this instinctive type of grasping. The 'I,'
however, manifests clearly when there are powerful conditions
for you to be happy or sad—such as when you are praised or crit-
icized. . . . *This* is the way the object of refutation will present itself
to you. Whenever this thinking manifests in any circumstance
making you glad, afraid, happy, or sad, and whenever this instinctive grasping develops strongly, you must examine on the
spot the way it appears to you.

Suppose two people are travelling side-by-side on the same
road, each seeing their companion out of the corner of their eye.
This illustrates the following. While your mind continues to act
instinctively, and while the object to be refuted presents itself to
you, you must examine the instinctive mode of appearance of this
object with a minute part of your mind. If this mind examining
the mode of appearance of the 'I' is too strong, you will lose your

grip on a part of the 'I,' and this part will become unclear. (Pabongka Rimpoche, pp. 686–87)

I would like to suggest that the act of reading provides a particularly
opportune circumstance for catching the illusory self unawares, of
catching the illusion of the self and the illusion of the text while both are
distracted by looking at each other. Rilke's "Archaic Torso of Apollo" is
a thematic allegory of this moment of insight in the apprehension of a
work of art:

> We cannot know his legendary head
> with its eyes blank as ripening fruits. Yet
> the torso still burns with light from inside,
> like a torch, in which his gaze, now reduced,
>
> shines forth with all its strength. Elsewise,
> the curve of the chest would not dazzle you, nor
> a smile shoot through the quiet thighs and hips
> to the dark center where the sex once hung.
>
> Elsewise this stone would look defaced
> beneath the lucent descent of the shoulders,
> would not shine like the pelt of a wild beast;
>
> would not, from all its edges,
> blaze like a star: there is no place here
> that does not see you. You must change your life.
> ("Archaïscher Torso Apollos," my translation)

The perceiver or reader is reflected in the *doppelganger* of art, broken
into the metonymies of plastic representation. Where, among all these
carefully, mimetically shaped parts, is the imputed identity we call
"Apollo," after the long-dead Greeks? Nowhere so much as in the missing head, the spaces left by the pieces of the statue that have broken
away, truncation and incompletion imposed by time as a signature, a
final, anonymous closure (which abolishes, violently, the closure of
wholeness the artist had wrought) on the work. It is the truncation of
the art that points to the (merely) imputed integrity of the perceiver, as
it recalls the final authority of impermanence, and the lack of clear distinction between the object perceived and the perceiving subject. The

emptiness of the gaze, real or imaginary, is what constitutes the essence, the instant and the emptiness of art. Rilke's poem is an especially dense and obvious corroboration of Pabongka Rinpoche's advice, but the same insight may occur in the reading of any text—the abrupt seizure of insight, or a creeping, quiet sense that what we see or hear, or read, is an other self looking back, as in this passage from a story by Flannery O'Connor:

> She sat on the step, clutching the banister spoke while the breath came back into her a thimbleful at a time and the stairs stopped seesawing. She opened her eyes and gazed down into the dark hole, down to the very bottom . . .
>
> Then she recognized the feeling again, a little roll. It was as if it were not in her stomach. It was as if it were out nowhere in nothing, out nowhere, resting and waiting, with plenty of time. (p. 84)

This is literature as a kind of tantra (a Sanskrit word meaning weft or continuum). Tantric practice involves using desires and pleasures, including fleshly ones, to achieve enlightenment. This entails meditation and visualization while engaged in pleasurable activity. In the West, we are accustomed to thinking of Buddhism only in terms of its Therarada form, which tends to be ascetic and monastic, and defined in terms of denial of fleshly pleasure. But the tantric and Mahayana paths are very different.

> The Vajrayana [tantric Buddhism] places great emphasis on the transformation of objects so that rather than energizing the three poisons of ignorance, attachment, and anger within you, they energize bliss instead. . . .
>
> Many Westerners think that it must be painful to understand samsara the way it's explained in Buddhism: "Buddhism says that life is suffering; that means there's no way out!" It seems that Buddhist philosophy and meditation were created for the express purpose of making people miserable! That's a completely wrong attitude; they don't understand what they really need. (Yeshe, pp. 124–25)

Literary activity, reading and writing, are the closest thing we have in the West to the active and pleasurable visualizations of Tantra, in which

"Emptiness is not reified as a lifeless void, but as the soft, jeweled womb of compassionate embodiment, life expanding to give freedom and bliss to others, boundless life" (Thurman 1988, p. 131). To be sure, literary pursuits do not necessarily lead to "enlightenment"; without some guidance, and some understanding, they are only confusing—as for the graduate student whose question I have been trying to answer. The philosophy of the Middle Way provides a vehicle for accommodating various "theories" and "readings" within the understanding of the mind and the text as formless continuums defined ultimately only by emptiness. It also embraces ethical considerations, by contrast with some Buddhist thinkers who have asserted that since phenomena are not ultimately real, ethical behaviors such as compassion are unnecessary—in a manner reminiscent of some Western deconstructionists who have taken an apparently nihilistic position with regard to political and ethical issues (though even extreme skepticism, I would argue, can be a very powerful ethical position).

According to the Middle Way Consequence School, this view remains mired in dualism. The boddhisattva who has realized emptiness also knows the nondistinction of phenomena from emptiness, and acts in a way that accepts conventional reality as impermanent but not different from ultimate truth.

> Nowadays, some who are vain about having high views say that phenomena are only mistaken appearances and take them to be utterly non-existent, like the child of a barren woman; then they hold that non-attention to anything is the supreme practice. They do not have even the scent of a Consequentialist in them. (Sopa, p. 320)

This is like the deconstructionist critic who claims that, because his or her reading inscribes within it the inevitable epistemological failure of all others, any other way of reading is therefore false and superfluous. Even at its best, deconstruction, as we have seen, retains a certain Cartesian grasping, clinging to the Master Subject. The late Paul de Man was, I think, approaching the Middle Way when he proposed rhetoric as the best system for talking about literature, inasmuch as rhetoric is *empty form* and subsumes all other "methods" of reading.

> Technically correct rhetorical readings may be boring, monotonous, predictable and unpleasant, but they are irrefutable. They

are also totalizing (and potentially totalitarian) for since the structures and functions they expose do not lead to the knowledge of an entity (such as language) but are an unreliable process of knowledge production that prevents all entities, including linguistic entities, from coming into discourse as such, they are indeed universals, consistently defective models of language's impossibility to be a model language. They are, always in theory, the most elastic theoretical and dialectical model to end all models and they can rightly claim to contain within their own defective selves all the other defective models of reading-avoidance, referential, semiological, grammatical, performative, logical, or whatever. They are theory and not-theory at the same time, the universal theory of the impossibility of theory. (De Man 1986, p. 19)

But what is rhetoric, or trope (which is what de Man means by rhetoric)?—if not substitution, calling something by a name not its own, for no name is "proper," naturally "attached" to any thing. Even the thematic, an ontological category de Man tended to oppose to the rhetorical, is simply another kind of rhetoric. All uses and forms of language, in and out of literature, are rhetorical; but there is more: *so are all forms of knowing*. In fact, the mind is not distinct from the text, and both are empty forms; there are many truths in each and more still in both together. On the level of conventional reality, compassion is as indispensable as wisdom, and not even different from it.

Tibetan Buddhist practice is admittedly very different from Zen. The former advocates a gradual path to enlightenment, which can involve conceptual study (this is a kind of meditation, too) as well as other forms of meditation, while the latter ostensibly admits only direct apprehension of the nature of mind. But, again, as the work of recent scholars such as Heine and Faure, and those of the Japanese school of Critical Buddhism have shown, traditional, serious Zen practice does not proscribe scholarly or literary activity. Literary analysis and production, playing with words, were for Dogen Zenji however an advanced, not a preliminary practice.

Both traditions embrace the Middle Way, and both therefore offer something to the Western student of literature. "The Buddha's teaching of the Dharma relies on the two realities: the social, superficial reality, and the reality of Ultimate Import," as Nagarjuna said. I propose that our teaching of literature should do the same.

There *are* such persons as "Buddhas," they *do* teach, and they do not teach only One Reality, or one unreality. They teach two realities; a relative one that is superficial—lying on the surface—and social—conventionally structured by culture, which shapes consciousness through language; and an Ultimate Absolute that is profound, transcendent, yet real, *knowable*, and hence of supreme import, being ultimately liberative and transformative. "Those who do not discern the difference between these two realities do not understand the profound, the principle of the Buddha-Doctrine." Any conflation of the two, misapprehension that samsara is *just* Nirvana, or that Nirvana is *just* samsara, misses the profound principle, the Thatness of the Teaching of Enlightenment. "Without employing the conventional, the Ultimate is not taught. Without understanding the Ultimate Reality, Nirvana is not attained." The most important communication is teaching. The most important subject of teaching is Ultimate Reality, as it is most important to know it; for its knowledge results in the attainment of liberation, Nirvana, the highest bliss, which is the best thing that can happen to a sentient being. The relative world is there, but so is its transcendence, and the path of liberation is indeed proclaimed to be viable. (Thurman 1984, pp. 156–57; quotations are from Nagarjuna, *Wisdom, Fundamental Central Way Verses*)

The Ultimate Reality, of course, is not different from the relative, superficial ones: it is their emptiness.

We need not fear theory, or take it too seriously. All theories are empty, like all texts, and all readers. Two things are always true of every text: it is always the same, no matter who enacts or reads it, or how; and it is always entirely new and different every time and at every instant that it is read, whether by the same person or not. The same is true of us as we read, for the texts enact us as we enact them. And the same is true of the theories by which we make claims to Ultimate Reality in and through our readings: all theories are viable because all are void.

So finally, the truth about literary texts cannot be stated, but only performed. The only true meaning in a poem is another poem, and poems are rewritten every time they are read well. A good reading, using this theory or that, may be perfectly true, and in the instant in which it occurs, exhaustively so, but it can never be definitive. All readings are limited by their temporal and circumstantial specificity. The circumstances must be defined in terms of the individual (another kind of text) being read by the text even as he or she reads it, and neither text nor reader is ever exactly the same twice. Time makes sure that this is no less true when the identity of the reader and the text being read remain constant. The "truth" of literature, in this perspective, is that it is not a thing, but a way—or ways, whose meaning must reside in the ever-repeated act of performance.

3

The Karmic Text:
Buddhism and Translation

"Unity" is not contemplated in terms of any metaphysical principle but is, instead, acted out.

—Hee-Jin Kim
Dogen Kigen: Mystical Realist

The very act of interpretation, then, involves the whole person, the body-mind unified through intensity of focus and held *(ji)* together in the personal act *(gyo)*, the continuous practice *(gyoji)* inseparable from enlightenment.

—Thomas P. Kasulis
"The Incomparable Philosopher: Dogen on How to Read the Shobogenzo"

Virtually all writing about translation sooner or later describes it as a conundrum, an epistemological impasse of and in language, but beyond words to describe. When we translate literature, a new text is produced from an "original" one—though, in the case of some older texts, the original, as in the case of the Christian synoptic gospels, may be a translation already. Translation is about texts coming from texts, about texts being transmuted into different media. It raises questions such as: What is a text if not the aggregates of words that constitute it? If a text is only those, how can it be translated into other words, even ones of approximately the same "meaning," and remain the same text? If it does not remain the same text, why call it by the same title? Why call it a "translation"? Yet if something is there beyond the precise linguistic configuration of the "original," what is it and can it be transferred from one language to another, one text to another?

Obviously these are questions that go to the heart of literary textuality and of communication. They are also questions about the nature of individual being. What is an individual consciousness, or a mind? Is it anything beyond the aggregate of physical parts that comprise a human being? Yet it cannot be isolated in any one of those parts. Why is a brain in a jar not the same as a living, working brain? To answer "Because the former is dead and the latter alive" is merely a tautology, answering the question with a question. Buddhist philosophy has formulated answers to these questions regarding human existence. Might these not be useful, even if only as analogies, in understanding the process of translation? Might we not consider translation as a kind of literary metempsychosis, or transmigration of literary being? Before trying to do so, we must first examine the conundrum as we in the West have lived it.

> Translation is a disturbing craft because there is precious little certainty about what we are doing, which makes it so difficult in this age of fervent belief and ideology, this age of greed and screed.
>
> —Gregory Rabassa
> "No Two Snowflakes Are
> Alike: Translation as Metaphor"

> All poetry is translation.
>
> —Harold Bloom
> *Poetry and Repression*

> I want translations with copious footnotes, footnotes reaching up like skyscrapers to the top of this or that page so as to leave only the gleam of one textual line between commentary and eternity.
>
> —Vladmiir Nabokov
> "Problems of Translation:
> *Onegin* in English"

> The human mind can do nothing but translate; all its activity consists of just that.
>
> —A. W. Schlegel
> *Translating Literature*

Presently available literature on translation is of two kinds: practical and theoretical. Exemplary of the first are works such as *The Task of the Translator,* edited by John Biguenet and Rainer Schulte, in which several highly respected translators talk about translation mostly in practical terms, describing the difficulties of specific texts and the ways in which they overcame them. Donald Frame, of all the contributors to the Biguenet/Schulte volume, comes closest to eschewing any remarks that are not practical in nature: "In all these pages I have dealt almost solely with the problems I have seen in my practice of translation and my attempts to solve them or at least cope with them" (p. 92). Everyone else confesses to a sense of profoundly impractical angst, try as they may to remain calmly matter-of-fact. "In the pages that follow," begins William Weaver, for example, "I have tried to fix on paper the stages of an elusive process: the translation of an Italian text into English." He does so elegantly and instructively, but he is forced to admit the limitations of what can be told.

> If someone asks me how I translate, I am hard put to find an answer. I can describe the physical process: I make a very rapid first draft, put it aside for a while, then go over it at a painfully slow pace, pencil—and eraser—in hand. But that is all outside. Inside, the job is infinitely complex, and what's more, it varies from one author to another. I wish I could describe the thrilling tingle I feel when something seems, finally, to have come right. I prefer not to dwell on the sinking sensation felt when it is obvious that something is dreadfully wrong. (p. 118)

Every one of the translators in this volume confesses a similar, often anguished sense of the impossibility of what each does, and of the simultaneous and epistemologically similar impossibility of adequately describing how they do this thing that it is not possible to do. Both things get done—but not, all agree, properly, finally, adequately. Or perhaps adequately but not perfectly.

It is odd that the merely practical, pedagogical format of these essays almost immediately forces the most accomplished translators to admissions of epistemological impasse and failure. Edward Seidensicker, translator of Murasaki Shikibu's *The Tale of Genji,* writes wearily, with a very Japanese sense of resignation, that "Japanese is, in a way, somewhat untranslatable. . . . Let us only say that there are difficulties, and that translation, as Allen Tate said of criticism, is forever impossible and forever necessary" (p. 153). Margaret Sayers Peden says that "All translations should be followed by a blank page. That blank page awaits the ideal translation" (p. 27). Gregory Rabassa adds that "The translator can never be sure of himself, he must never be" (p. 12).

Willis Barnstone's *The Poetics of Translation* is in the same vein but more historical. He makes the obligatory confession, like everyone else: "Perfect translatability is impossible. Everything is untranslatable" (p. 42). Less typically, Barnstone, as a translator of poetry, is interested in the way in which translations serve poet/translators as "dress rehearsal" for more purely "creative" activity. Strangely, he notes, the "lesson of translation" is not in the original being translated, but in the very act of translation itself, and in the "secondary" text it generates.

> Translation is the teacher of poets. The lessons lie not, however, in the source language but in the target language, not primarily in the source books, but in the poet's own versions. These versions are instigated by the activity of translation; what is sovereign, however, is the product of that activity, their own work in their translated versions. Through the experience of translation, and of subsequent self-imitation based on foreign poems in their own versions that become their models and instructors in their own poems, poets have developed as poets, and, immersed in their foreignness, have also established an international tradition in their own languages and national literatures. (p. 113)

If this is *how* translation teaches, then we are faced with a daunting question of *what* it teaches—which goes to the heart of what a text is. It is not enough to say that translation teaches poets how to write their own poems. That too would be a tautology, and reopen, at a profounder level, the question of how.

Searching for a reply to his own questions, Barnstone is led immediately to questions of the sacred, of the translation of sacred texts. He devotes most of the rest of his book to the way in which the sacred text we call the Bible—"the [Western] world's major paper monument to translation" (p. 137)—has evolved through translation and as translation, mutating itself repeatedly, through many different languages and translators, many of whom acted more from ideological/political motivation than by divine inspiration.

> So the Greek synoptic Gospels, derived from each other and from an earlier Semitic text, in fact constituted an attempt to usurp the affective word of God from the Hebrew Bible and the Jews, just as

Jesus, through the drama of his human appearance and his agony, had usurped and diminished the role and authority of Yahweh . . .

Each new translation of the Bible, whether that of Jerome, Luther, or the scholars of King James, rebelliously attempts to retrieve and possess the lost word. In doing so, the translation assumes a new authority, endowing its created word with the glory and magnificence of the original—and indeed surpassing the "corrupt" original. In these translations—albeit of the holiest texts of the Judeo-Christian world—the second text becomes the original. (p. 136)

Throughout the history of biblical translation, there has been a fierce and often vicious dialectic between translation and antitranslation, always politically motivated, though nearly always masquerading as sacred authority.

The politics of religion, particularly of Christianity, in regard to translation have always been ambiguous. On the one hand, there is the sacred view that holds to the process of entropy, the idea that any passage between languages implies waste, corruption, and fundamental loss. On the other, there is the constant didactic and messianic need to spread the word of God to potential converts, for which Bible translation is an indispensable tool. (p. 43)

The same ambiguity characterizes much of the academic attitude toward literary translation, now and in the past.

Despite repeated and sometimes inept translation, and even, very early on, the unspeakable indignity of translation by committee, the Bible has retained its unquestioned position in every Western culture and language as the sacred text; and ironically, for being the case *par excellence* of textual translation/text-as-translation, no one but scholars really consider the Bible as a work in translation. Most practicing Christians consider the Bible in *their* language—or one of them—to be a "divinely" inspired book. Barnstone turns an anecdotal history of the Bible as translation into a useful occasion for many personal observations on the process of translation, but he never finds an answer to the fundamental questions he raises about what translation is, and what texts are. The unsaid premise, of Barnstone and all the contributors to *The Task of the Translator* seems to be: *I can't tell you, but maybe I can show you.*

Finally, Barnstone comes up against the most "sacred" modern text on the theory of translation, Walter Benjamin's "The Task of the Translator." The appearance of this text within Barnstone's discussion heralds the advent of the second type of writing about translation (the first was "practical"), the more directly and admittedly theoretical kind. Even so, all Barnstone manages to do is point out the ways in which Benjamin's text remains a conundrum, despite the efforts of readers as gifted as Paul de Man to make sense of it. "The more specifically one presses these analogies," Barnstone writes, "the less certain the correct referents are, and the less lucid and more ambivalent becomes the fragmentary analogy that Benjamin offers us" (p. 250).

Benjamin's text, much like hermetic scripture or mystical poetry, speaks in runes, paying only a minimum of formal homage to linear thought, straining at the generic limits of the essay. This is so because Benjamin believes that "language and revelation are one" (p. 82). He expresses better than anyone else the danger inherent to translation, acknowledged by virtually all good translators: "The gates of a language thus expanded and modified may slam shut and enclose the translator with silence" (p. 81). Benjamin is rapturously preoccupied with something he calls "Pure Language," with which it is the unique property of translation to bring us into intimate contact.

> To turn the symbolizing into the symbolized, to regain pure language fully formed in the linguistic flux, is the tremendous and only capacity of translation. In this pure language—which no longer means or expresses anything but is, as expressionless and creative Word, that which is meant in all languages—*all information, all sense, and all intention finally encounter a stratum in which they are destined to be extinguished.* (p. 80; my emphasis)

The only certain thing of possible practical value that can be extracted from all this is that "Benjamin decrees [the relation of the original to the translation] as dialectical" (Barnstone, p. 243).

With Joseph Graham's collection, *Difference in Translation*, we enter the realm of avowedly pure theory, though practical considerations cannot be avoided here, any more than theoretical ones were by the avowedly untheoretical practitioners before. Graham's volume provides a forum in which a number of prominent deconstructionist critics, including Jacques Derrida, mull over translation as a strange case in which theory and practice cannot be clearly distinguihed. Aptly, several of the contributors to this volume use the translation of works by Jacques Derrida—the founder of deconstruction—in the same way that Barnstone uses the translation of the Bible, as paradigmatic instances of translation. This is justified because

> Derrida's entire philosophic enterprise, indeed, can be seen as an analysis of the translation process at work in every text. In studying the *differance* of signification, Derrida follows the misfires, losses, and infelicities that prevent any given language from being *one*. Language, in fact, can only exist in the space of its own foreignness to itself. But all of Western philosophy has had as its aim to repress that foreignness, to take a text that is "as little German as it would be English" and to make it into the transparent expression of a great philosophic thought. Not only, however, is this self-differance the *object* of Derrida's attention: it is an integral part of the functioning of his own écriture. (pp. 146–47)

Most of the contributors to Graham's book also agree that translation is a perfect metaphor for understanding, and for *knowing*, insofar as knowledge entails an inevitable linguistic aspect. Most agree that translation inevitably misconstrues the source text, sometimes violently, sometimes fortuitously, often both at once. As Barbara Johnson writes, "It is thus precisely the way in which the original text is always already an impossible translation that renders translation impossible" (p. 146). This is often, as Philip Lewis says, a case of trying to make clear in the translation what is not clear in the source text, something that most conscientious translators are guilty of doing at one time or other, and which Derrida's translators are virtually obliged to do. According to Lewis,

> the salient feature of the translator's introduction, which reaffirms the value of natural, intelligible, idiomatic English precisely by setting it off against Derrida's tortuous, precious, language-straining French, is that the translator begins by pointing out quite explicitly that the essay, through its analyses and arguments, contests the very criteria and suppositions that nonetheless govern his translation. . . .
>
> The translation thus tends to sap the strength of the thesis it restates by blocking off its enactment or enforcement by the

statement and thereby allowing the contested values [the values of the "transparency" of the word] to prevail unshaken in the fabric of the very discourse [Derrida's] that purports to contest them. (pp. 57–58)

And it is a fact acknowledged by Lewis, Johnson, and by Derrida himself that translation impinges irrevocably on the original text. The original is altered, its primacy in part usurped by the act of translation, only to be restituted at the cost of an uncertain distinction between original and translation. But this, according to Johnson, merely enacts explicitly a phenomenon already implicit in the source text ("original"), itself already a "translation" of experience, thought, or both.

Derrida himself, in the essay he contributes to close Graham's book, returns to exactly where Barnstone ended in his very different volume: to Benjamin's "Task of the Translator." He concludes that

[Truth] is not the representational correspondence between the original and the translation, nor even the primary adequation between the original and some object or signification exterior to it. Truth would be rather the *pure language* in which the meaning and the letter no longer dissociate. . . .

The sacred surrenders itself to translation, which devotes itself to the sacred. The sacred would be nothing without translation, and translation would not take place without the sacred; the one and the other are inseparable. In the sacred text "the meaning has ceased to be the divide for the flow of language and for the flow of revelation." It is the absolute text because in its event it communicates nothing, it says nothing that would make sense beyond the event itself. That event melds completely with the act of language, for example with prophecy. It is literally the literality of its tongue, "pure language." And since no meaning bears detaching, transferring, transporting, or translating into another tongue as such (meaning), it commands right away the translation that it seems to refuse. (p. 204)

That is, the most sacred, "truest" language is that in which meaning and letter perfectly coincide, a perfect realization of MacLeish's poetic injunction that "A poem should not mean, but be." "Speaking in tongues," divine gibberish, would be an example. Prophecy by definition enacts its own truth. And because it is babel, opaque, because it refuses the dualism of letter and meaning and therefore confounds understanding in the conventional sense, to understand, we shuttle back and forth betweeen what appears to us as the letter and what it appears to "signify," for without that apparent dualism there is no understanding, and so prophecy compels exegesis, deciphering, commentary, translation, all the things it seemed at first to render moot and impossible. This at least is Derrida's reading of Benjamin.

His intellectual, if not spiritual brother, the late Paul de Man, also tried to read (to "translate") Benjamin's text. In de Man's reading, "pure language" is the phenomenon of intralingualism devoid of even the pretense to grounding in some extralingual referent. Translation is in this respect like critical theory; both expose in the source text ("original") an instability that may not be immediately evident.

> Both criticism and translation are caught in the gesture which Benjamin calls ironic, a gesture which undoes the stability of the original by giving it a definitive, canonical form in the translation or in the theorization . . . That the original was not purely canonical is clear from the fact that it demands translation; it cannot be definitive since it can be translated. . . . The translation canonizes, freezes an original and shows in the original a mobility, an instability, which at first one did not notice. The act of critical, theoretical reading performed by a critic like Friedrich Schlegel and performed by literary theory in general—by means of which the original work is not imitated or reproduced but is to some extent *put in motion*, de-canonized, questioned in a way which undoes its claim to canonical authority—is similar to what a translator performs. (1986, pp. 82–83; my emphasis)

De Man comes nearer the essence of Benjamin than Benjamin himself, than anyone else who has ever tried to read/rewrite/"translate" "The Task of the Translator" when he (de Man) suggests that translation reveals to us our alienation, and our suffering, in language. Translation and critical theory, according to de Man, reveal a fundamental literary corollary of the first of the Four Noble Truths of Buddhism (Life is impermanent and characterized by suffering):

> What translation does, by reference to the fiction or hypothesis of a pure language devoid of the burden of meaning, is that it

implies—in bringing to light what Benjamin calls "die Wehen des eigenen"—the suffering of what one thinks of as one's own—the suffering of the original language. We think we are at ease in our own language, we feel a coziness, familiarity, a shelter in the language we call our own, in which we think that we are not alienated. What the translation reveals is that this alienation is at its strongest in our relation to our own original language, that the original language within which we are engaged is disarticulated in a way which imposes upon us a particular alienation, a particular suffering. (1986, p. 84)

The reasons for this pathos, for this *Wehen*, for this suffering, are specifically linguistic . . . The text about translation is itself a translation, and the untranslatability which it mentions about itself inhabits its own texture and will inhabit anybody who in his turn will try to translate it, as I am now trying, and failing, to do. The text is untranslatable; it was untranslatable for the translators who tried to do it [and who over and over again, in de Man's reading, are shown to have gotten Benjamin's very literal meaning quite wrong], it is untranslatable for the commentators who talk about it, it is an example of what it states, it is a *mise en abîme* in the technical sense, a story within the story of its own statement. (1986, p. 86)

Thus to read Benjamin accurately, one can only fail outright in the way that he failed, that his texts and his translators failed. De Man's superiority over other readers of Benjamin is in the directness with which he confronts, and embraces that failure.

Yet what is this failure? "Failure" is not by any means a neutrally descriptive word. The term, like "loss" (which immediately evokes a stream of pejoratives, beginning with "loser") condemns one outcome by implicitly comparing it to another, more desired or desirable one; something else *should* have happened. Failure, more even than loss, implies *blame*, that the negative outcome is the direct result of some decision or act that could have been avoided. Yet, in the terms in which de Man elucidates it, Benjamin's failure was preordained and there is nothing anyone could have done to avoid it. Why then choose a word that is negatively prescriptive and even moralistic? There is, as de Man says, a willful pathos in the choice of such a word. What can be the phenomenon under scrutiny, capable of compelling such a negative characterizaton from even a reader as (putatively) dispassionate as de Man?

The epistemological phenomenon that all of de Man's and Derrida's work decribes and must enact by describing, as they say, is a failure, a "bad thing." (Derrida, though more playful—and more opaque—in his morbidity, is also fond of such words as failure [*échec*], rupture, breakage [*brisure*].) The implications are interesting: Derrida and de Man would appear to agree with their critics that *différance*, the nonintegrity of texts and knowledge, is a *negative phenomenon*, even a catastrophe. Both remain within the bounds of a Judeo-Christian, moralistic Cartesianism, which reads the inability of its own dualisms to sustain themselves under close scrutiny, scientific or logical, as infused with pathos, a "tragic," disrupting force. This is where we are led by close observation of the process—theory and practice—of translation.

Theory on the subject would then appear to mask a certain (sublimated) sentimentality, and all of the nontheoretical works similarly bemoan (1) the failure of all translation to really fulfill its promise, and (2) the failure of any talk about translation to adequately describe the process, even in modestly practical terms. All assume that they were supposed to say something other than what they do or are able to say. This may be because we in the West are haunted by a certain idea of what textuality is supposed to be. We remain mired in the notion of text as a definitive, self-contained totality, even if we know—like Derrida and de Man—that this is a fiction.

Perhaps the only way out of such nostalgia is in a different, non-Cartesian, non-Judeo-Christian, non-Western idea of what textuality is. What, that is, is being transferred in the act of translation (or reading, or writing)? Meaning, signs, tropes—in the most radical instances, represented by Derrida and others, there seems nothing to transfer, and translation is impossible. Yet it occurs. Surely the hermeneutic model of the text, according to which we are literally transporting some kernel of essence when we translate, cannot hold up in the face of deconstruction, and yet the semiotic model of one-to-one decoding, without any hermeneutic grounding, cannot account for the extraordinary results obtained by William Weaver, translator of Italo Calvino, or Gregory Rabassa, translator of Gabriel Garcia Marquez.

Tibetan Buddhist scholasticism has developed an extremely subtle, complex epistemology of mind grounded principally in the idea that there is no mind-center.

It is tempting to see 'in mind' a center, a certain particular existent or kind of Pure Ego which stands in a common asymmetrical relation to all the 'mental events' which would be said to be states of a certain mind, or since 'mind' is itself an event, to see it as being of the same nature as the events which it holds together. Buddhist psychology, however, has generally rejected the assumption of a center in either sense. (Guenther, p. xxvi)

Still, there is a close relation between mind and its objects; they are not the same, but they are not entirely distinct.

Just as there is the knowable when there is knowing, there is knowing when there is the knowable. When both are unborn what is [there to be] understood? . . .

Consciousness occurs in dependence on the internal and external sense-fields. Therefore consciousness is empty, like mirages and illusions. Since Consciousness arises in dependence on a discernible object, the discernible does not exist [in itself]. Since [the conscious subject] does not exist without the discernible and consciousness, the conscious subject does not exist [by itself]. (Nagarjuna, pp. 29, 113)

"Seeing a thing belongs to mind"—mind is what happens when we see or generally perceive something—and "Seeing its specific characteristics belongs to a mental event." "Consciousness is a selecting awareness," and perception "is a distinct awareness of what is before the mind" (Guenther pp. 9, 14).

Contrary to the usual Western assumption, an important place is assigned to the written word, and to conceptual thought, within that system. (Conceptualization "is to know by association" [Guenther, p. 23]). Otherwise, there could scarcely be any place for art or literature. An even more important role is assigned to what is called "yogic direct perception," but direct perception of ultimate realities is possible only by prepatory exercise of conceptual thought. As Ann Klein has written, "Among religious philosophies of the world, it is not unusual to depict the human mind as capable of conceptual and nonconceptual experience; what is unusual, perhaps, is to harness the former in service of the latter" (pp. 206–7).

A Western literary theorist is likely to misconstrue what this means. It does *not* mean that the only valid theory of literature is materialistic or based on sensory perception, whether the latter is construed as subjective phenomena (as in phenomenology) or not. For the ultimate reality to be understood is the *emptiness* of material phenomena, the absence of any inherent existence to them, the fact of their existence as dependent arisings, as dependent on causes and circumstances. This applies above all to the self.

> The way that one becomes acquainted with the meaning of self-lessness is by carefully building up a mental image—an understanding—of the 'self' which is to be negated. One must identify the object of negation before one can know the non-affirming negative selflessness which is nothing other than the absence of that misconceived 'self.' Selflessness or emptiness is difficult to realize because its metaphysical space is a hair's breadth between the two overriding tendencies of any ordinary conceptual thought grappling with this concept: either nihilistically to eliminate objects entirely or to reify them too strongly. In the context of Sautrantika [the Sutra System of Tenets], one must be careful to delineate the substantially existent person negated from the insubstantial person which does exist. In other words, one must conceptually exclude the self-sufficient person without excluding the impermanent person that in Sautrantika is an ultimate truth. (pp. 207–8)

So that conceptual (which includes literary or linguistic) knowing is indispensable to direct perception of subtle, nonapparent realities such as emptiness or selflessness.

Conceptual thought, on the one hand, is like a template; it arrives at an object through a negative process of elimination: "A thought apprehending pot sees an image which is the opposite of that which is non-pot" (Napper 1980, pp. 34–35). Direct perception, on the other hand, is a "collective engager" because it engages all the unique aspects of a given, impermanent object at one moment: "All those things that are established with the object, abide with it, and disintegrate when it does—such as the individual particles of the object, its impermanence, momentariness, and so forth, appear to that consciousness" (Napper 1980, p. 34). However, "An ordinary direct perceiver is unable to *notice* all of these, but a yogic direct perceiver can see and ascertain them" (p. 31). Conceptual (literary) knowing is of extreme importance in the progression from ordinary to yogic direct perception.

Ways of knowing that are accomplished through the use of language—reading or learning from a teacher, for instance—are generally described in Tibetan Buddhist (Gelukba[1]) epistemology as a form of conceptual consciousness called a "correctly assuming consciousness." In the process of reading, we impute or assume objects—persons, situations, places—by a process of elimination determined by the words the author has written. When the text says goldfish bowl, we arrive at a mental image of this object, not a direct perception of a real bowl with real water and real goldfish in it. Our mental image is formed by the use of a kind of mental "template," by which we eliminate everything that is not bowl, and everything that is not goldfish bowl. This leaves a number of possibilities for distinct size, shape, material (plastic or glass), whether or not actually containing goldfish, and so on, based on all our actual direct perceptions of such objects, and our memory of these. The literary/conceptual perception of this object involves a number of mind continuums that are memories of direct perceptions. The conceptual image we are left with, and which will constitute the "fictive" reality of the text, is based on these continuums or memories, which are peculiar to each individual reader, though always referring to the same real object.

So a textual scene differs from a real one in that it is only negatively known by the use of mental "templates"; the aspect of each object is determined by elimination of everything that is not the object or has not been the object in actual experience. It is part of what defines literature that we are to "color in" this simulated or conceptual scene, and to think of it as we would of one directly perceived. In translation, we then work backward, from this "template" or "silhouette" conceptual reality, to corresponding words in a different language from that of the source text. The words of the translation evoke certain "templates" in a reader as well, which will be similar but not identical owing to the different linguistic medium as well as to the unique memories of object-experience of each reader.

Except for the additional variable of a new language, and for being filtered through the mind-continuum of a second "author" (the translator), the translation is no different from the original; every reader's direct perceptions of objects and situations, and memories of them, will be different. In this way the text and all its variants, readings, and translations are a continuum in which readers, translators, and the author—each at the instant of reading or writing, with all the continu-ums of memory and thought that comprise his or her consciousness—are subsumed.

If the textual object or situation is one the reader has never experi-enced directly, then it is apprehended only as a "term-generality," from which a "meaning-generality" must be inferred, either from context, on the basis of similar direct experience, from other texts (a dictionary, for instance), or all of these; in the Tibetan system, when this occurs it is called an "inferential cognizer." Whether grounded in inference or memory of direct experience, or some combination of the two, all liter-ary knowing is conceptual.

It is peculiar to literature that we are asked to think of textual (conceptual) realities *as though* they were no different from directly ex-perienced ones. This means that literature asks us to forget or disregard the difference between a conceptual and a direct perception. From a theoretical point of view, it focuses attention on the ways in which con-ceptual and direct perceptions are alike, and the ways in which they must remain different. It is essential in this respect that Gelukba Bud-dhist thought does *not* exclude objects from thought consciousness.

> Existent or 'real' objects can actually be apprehended through the medium of an image. . . . it is precisely because the image pertains to *both* the thought consciousness perceiving it and the external referent object that such an appearance is known as a meaning-*generality*. It thus partakes of both the thought consciousness and the represented object." (Klein, pp. 209–10)

That a conceptual/linguistic knower can only know negatively does not mean that it knows nothing about real objects.

> The Gelukbas note that an appearance of a pot to thought is not as clear as an appearance of a pot to direct perception, but they would not agree with [those] who use this reason to deny that words relate to external reality because they do not evoke the "full-blooded experience of the objects to which they refer." (Klein, p. 210)

In other words, "although that which appears to thought—for exam-ple, an appearance of the elimination of all that is not pot—is indeed only an image and not the actual object, the determined object of that consciousness, that which is understood through the image, is just that object itself" (Napper 1980, p. 30). This means that in the process of reading, though we do not directly experience objects, we do gain knowledge of objects. Reading and translation are a matter of transferring knowledge about real objects, at the same time that they transfer no direct or positive consciousness of objects.

Conceptual knowledge and direct sense perception are thus seen in the Gelukba—the most highly developed Tibetan theoretical system —as complementary. Literary/conceptual "knowledge" can directly and profoundly affect the way in which we directly perceive objects. Having read Proust, for instance, we can never again experience linden tea and madeleine cakes in quite the same way, much less love or time.

> On the one hand, sense direct perception is extolled as the nonerroneous consciousness par excellence, to which all of the coessential properties of its object appear. On the other hand, sense perception is not considered powerful enough, as it were, to combat the reificatory tendencies of the mind, here called *external and internal error*. In short, sense perception simply cannot *understand* all that appears to it.

> The reificatory errors can be combatted, not by a mind that passively accepts all of the qualities the object presents to it (as sense perception does), but by a form of knowledge that distinguishes between these qualities and brings to sharp focus one particular property, such as impermanence. (Cabezon, p. 129)

Literary reading is a particularly effective means of combatting the reificatory error, the tendency to think of perceived objects as permanent and inherently existing, because it first asks us to deliberately blur the distinction between conceptual thought and sense perception. We are asked to perform the former while pretending to be performing the latter. By momentarily pretending that they are the same, literary knowing, reading, contaminates each—conceptual knowing and direct perception—by the other and questions the premises of each from the vantage point of the other. When we read about a goldfish bowl, all our memories of direct perceptions of goldfish bowls are evoked, and all our future direct perceptions of goldfish bowls are affected by this literary and conceptual image to the extent that the literary experience moves or affects us, and affects the way we ascertain this object henceforth. When we translate or study literature in a conceptual (theoretical) way—that is, when we engage the text as text, not just as a pleasurable illusion (an artificial "window on the real")—our attention must be drawn to the way in which real perception and conceptual knowing are complementary, and thus to the emptiness of object phenomena, as well as the negative nature of conceptual knowledge.

Texts, because they involve purely conceptual and negative ways of knowing, are empty in a specific, limited sense, in addition to the general one in which all phenomena are understood to be empty. Literary texts make us aware of this specific emptiness by requiring us to overlook it, by insisting that we must think what the text represents to us as though it were really before our eyes, and ears, and other senses. In this way, the negative (silhouette or template) aspect of texts, the conceptuality/fictiveness of literary scenes and persons, points directly to the emptiness of the real, of real scenes and persons, when these are directly experienced. Some texts may do this more effectively than others. Proust does it particularly well by emphasizing the mutability, the impermanence of his characters' desires and personalities. So he directly points out the emptiness of real persons and objects, of our own selves. But he only exploits a possibility that is innate, and implicit, to all literary experience.

If we can experience conceptual images as though they were real—by reading works of literature—in the same way and with at least some of the same force that we experience the real, then there must be something like the emptiness of words, of conceptual images, which invests real objects. In the Yogachara or Mind Only System, this is expressed in the assertion that "phenomena exist as 'mere imputations by name and thought'" (Cabezon, p. 194). The more self-aware literary experience becomes, the more it is capable of inducing insight into the true nature of reality (emptiness), "which cannot be directly cognized" (Klein, p. 214) without such conceptual preparation. "The Madhyamika system describes a yogic direct perceiver's direct and nondualistic cognition of emptiness as being like fresh water poured into fresh water; subject and object—the mind and emptiness—are fused as if one." In literary experience, the reader's consciousness becomes nondistinct from its object (the text), from the conceptual reality imputed by means of the text, and from the object reality outlined by the conceptual one. Literary conceptual knowing becomes deliberately, consciously confused with direct perception, and thus provides a simulacrum of mind-emptiness, subject-object fusion, an intimation of what yogic direct perception, the direct experience of nonduality, must be like. Such nondualistic experience paradoxically "epitomizes the very antithesis of conceptuality" and therefore of literary experience. However, this need not be paradoxical, for

> Emphatically, in this [the Gelukba] system, an understanding of emptiness is not seen as merely a matter of divorcing oneself from conceptuality. It requires patient cultivation of a specific under-standing which is then brought to the level of direct experience. As in the case of realizing impermanence, one progresses from a mere term-generality—dry words—to an apprehension of term and meaning-generalities as mixed, to an apprehension of only the meaning generality of emptiness itself. (Klein, pp. 214–15)

In the act of reading, reader and text are subsumed, like fresh water in fresh water. Translation, in the same way, enacts the translator's non-distinction from the source text. The translation is not distinct from ei-ther the translator's mind-continuum or the source text, in which the author's mind was momentarily, in a sequence of instants of writing—like an infinitely dense sequence of snapshots—subsumed ("poured"). All are like "fresh water poured into fresh water."

Emptiness and Derridean differance both deny the inherent exis-tence of objects and subjects of cognition.[2] However, with emptiness, this entails no rupture, no loss, no guilt, no epistemological conflagration—no de Manian "failure." This is true in part because the emptiness of phe-nomena means that there is no *difference* between nature and culture, nat-ural and artificial. Art is an extension of nature. There is nothing to be gained, in the Buddhist system, by playful obscurantism (Derrida) or lu-gubrious "failure" (de Man); nothing to subvert, and nothing to mourn. These tactics fall into the trap of what the Buddhist scholar Robert Thur-man calls "egocentric or reificatory skepticism," or skepticist absolutism.[3]

> The skeptic indeed transfers his instinctual absolutism to "noth-ing," making the mistake of thinking that lack of absolute basis is no basis at all, lack of absolutistic, privately grounded language is no language at all, lack of mathematically perfect logic is no logic at all, and so on. (1984, p. 99)[4]

If there is no epistemological failure, nor is there any need to posit a pure, utopic language (Benjamin). All language is empty, and therefore pure. "Emptiness is not a critique of logic, language, and validating cognition, but makes them all work properly by critiquing illogic, misuse of language, and delusive cognition" (Thurman, p. 157). There is nothing artificial or "perverse" about literature or translation; both emerge from nature, the *nature* of mind which is not distinct from the natural, rather than in opposition to it. Language is both "free from any supposed absolute substratum" and "a practical, conventional process, an ordinary activity of human beings, a 'form of life'" (Thurman 1984, p. 99). Written or spoken language might as well, then, be as clear as it can be. Its emptiness is not compromised by clarity. And it need not apologize for being empty, since emptiness is not "failure." All translation, and all reading, perfectly enact emptiness and dependent arising, whether or not they know it, and no matter how simple, crude, or obscure they may happen to be.

Texts are not unique as objects of conciousness, then, but they are exemplary. At the same time that they are objects of direct sense perception in the physical act of reading, they give rise to elaborate conceptual knowledge that suggests the emptiness of direct sense perception. By reading them, we come very close to a direct perception of the self's and the object's emptiness. So perhaps it is not surprising after all that something extraordinary should happen when great translators do their work, all Western theory, and bafflement, on the subject notwithstanding. Every translation is a meditation on emptiness and a performance of dependent arising; every great translation is extremely, palpably so. We should not be surprised, either, that there is no such thing as a definitive translation. John Ciardi's and Allen Mandelbaum's translations of Dante are both great works in English; so are Fitzgerald's, Lattimore's, and Mandelbaum's versions of Homer. Each is different, with a distinct literary voice and poetic virtues, yet all reenact the same source text.

"Unity" is not contemplated in terms of any metaphysical principle but is, rather, acted out (Kim, pp. 94–95). I have often resumed the ineffable aspect of translation by telling my students that it is like method acting, in which the actor becomes the role he is playing. This is very like tantric visualization in Vajrayana Buddhist practice.

There are . . . vajra identities of different bodies such as being a person with three faces and six arms, completely united with a consort, emanating light rays all around in different directions, and so forth. The yogin or yogini practices inhabiting such a dreamlike illusory body. (Thurman 1988, p. 124)

As translators, we must similarly *become the text as well as its author*, believing in our nondistinction from the text, from the consciousness that first performed it, in order to reenact the performance in a new linguistic medium. This is part of a rational, conceptual process involving research into the author's life, the form and history of the text, and so forth, but it must culminate in an instant of nonconceptual performance, or nondistinction from text and author—"pouring water into water." Despite the emphasis on the uniqueness of every individual reading and every instant of reading, this is not a "reader-response" approach, though it is certainly not "author-intentionalist," either.

> There is no "romantic" attempt to reconstitute the subjectivity or intention of the teacher via elaborate historical interpolation. Nor is there any idea of the nihilistically relativistic use of the text to constitute an entirely new personal meaning locked away in the subjectivity of the hearer. (Thurman 1988, p. 134)

Relativism and essentialism are both equally wrong. This does not prevent at least tantric texts—which our "literature" is most like—from being "multiply interpretable, intending that they resonate within . . . completely different subjectivities of persons" (Thurman 1988, p. 124).

Consciousness and text are essentially performances. They exist only as a succession of performances, of performative "events." Reading is a performance; so is translation and so is commentary. The latter two are like the "original" text in that they can be "performed" in turn. Writing itself is a performance. The beauty of writing, as countless writers have said in interviews and essays, is the immediacy, the *nondistinction* experienced in the instant of writing between the writer, the written, and the act. All are subsumed in performance. When the writing stops, that apparent nonduality also stops. A text unread is simply a physical object, paper and ink between two boards, glued together. Only in the act of reading or writing does a text exist as text, not latently but actually, and that existence is a function of its nondistinction from the reading or writing consciousness. This nondistinction occurs only virtually, in the virtual, ever displaced (forward, in time) instant of performance. It is like an actor's realization of a role: in the instant of performance the actor and the role are one thing, and the performance exists only in the virtual instant in which it takes place. In the theater, performance by actor and spectator is simultaneous, *but not identical*—rather only *virtually* the same, that is, nondistinct—whereas between the two performances of writing and reading a temporal delay necessarily occurs. After the actor's performance, it can only be remembered, or repeated on film or tape. The latter two are like written texts, however, having only latent existence until they are "performed" by a spectator.

To recapitulate: in the act of reading, writing, or both, text and consciousness perform each other. Each is performed, enacted, played out by the other. Both are involved—even subsumed—in a nondual continuum of mutual performance. The resulting product—poem, essay, scholarly commentary, translation—will reflect the beauty of the source text only to the extent that the enacted/enacting consciousness is capable of cognizing and reflecting beauty. Beauty is the experience of nonduality, of emptiness and dependent arising as one. Beauty is then (latent) *bodhi*, or enlightenment. Weak readings, poor translations, wearisome, useless commentaries are ones that betray beauty in this sense: they reflect no (even latent) sense of nonduality within the dualism that is language and understanding. Readings and translations, when they are aesthetically strong, and reflect an enlightened sense of nondistinction, are meditations in which we directly experience both emptiness and dependent arising. In the instant of reading, consciousness and the text occur simultaneously, each perfectly, mutually dependent on the other.

In Buddhist thought, human being comprises five skandas or aggregates: corporeality *(rupa)*, sensation, perception, mental formations, and consciousness. Texts can be said to comprise only three: form *(rupa)*, history (of all the performances of the text, which effectively recast it) and "meaning," which may be more or less differentiatable from form and history, but never absolutely so. Just as consciousness is an empty form and a formless continuum, so are texts. An unread text is only an object, its textuality latent. It is only realized as a continuum of all previous "performances," "events" of writing and reading, when it is read by someone. When we read, the consciousness that we think of as our "self" becomes nondistinct from that great continuum. So that no text is ever exactly the same twice. In the following passage, Lafcadio Hearn elegantly characterized the continuum of mind; I have changed his terms so that the same description applies to textuality.

The [Text] is only a temporary aggregate of countless illusions, a phantom-shell, a bubble sure to break. It is a creation of Karma,—or rather, . . . it *is* Karma. [Karma means simply "deed" in Sanskrit; it is aptly defined by Hearn as *"the integration of acts and thoughts"*; for texts, it is all the inflections of writing and rewriting, of previous readings, commentaries, translations.] To comprehend the statement fully, the reader should know that, in this Oriental philosophy, acts and thoughts are forces integrating themselves into material and mental phenomena, into what we call objective and subjective appearances. . . . The Karma [. . .] we call [text] is [meaning] and is [form];—both perpetually decay; both are perpetually renewed. From the unknown beginning, this double-phenomenon, objective and subjective, has been alternately dissolved and integrated [with each new reading or rewriting (translation)]: each integration is a birth; each [simultaneous] dissolution a death. There is no other birth or death but the birth and death of Karma in some form or condition. But at each re-birth the reintegration is never the reintegration of the identical phenomenon, but of another to which it gives rise,—as growth begets growth, as motion produces motion. So that the phantom—[text] changes not only as to form and condition, but as to actual [meaning] with every reembodiment. There is one Reality; but there is no permanent [text], no constant [meaning]: there is only phantom-[text], and phantom succeeds to phantom, as undulation to undulation, over the ghostly Sea of [reading and (re)writing]. And even as the storming of a sea is a motion of undulation, *not of translation*, [my emphasis; not of translation in the traditional *reified* Western sense]—even as it is the form of the wave only, not the wave itself, that [is moved or translated],—so in the passing of [texts from one mind or one language to another] there is only the rising and the vanishing of forms,—forms mental, forms material. The fathomless Reality does not pass. ("Nirvana," pp. 219–22)

Could it be said then, that texts receive karmic imprints from writers and readers? I would answer yes. A special kind of karma, conceptual in nature, but karma nonetheless. "The conceptual aggregate (samjna-skandha) is always operative to determine any state of consciousness," writes Robert Thurman. The anticonceptual bias of most Western Buddhist practictioners who "suffer from a variety of entrenched notions against the intellect and its role and power as a vehicle of liberation," is "particularly tragic," says Thurman,

> since by *conceptually* choosing to eschew concepts, they lose the flexibility of conceptual adaptation, and become stuck with whatever range of concepts their habit of mind deems comfortable. This dooms them as modern persons to the grievous error of taking the nihilistic reification of the metaphysical nothingness underlying materialist culture to be the emptiness or selflessness that is ultimate reality. (1984, p. 7)

This sort of error is a profound karmic force, though conceptual in nature. Great translators, and great readers—especially the ones who write their reading—might be said to create positive karma by their activity; the text is a receptacle for this positive karmic force. And it would also have to be true that readers and writers receive karmic imprints from texts. This has long been assumed to be the case in Tibetan Buddhism. Not only does it make sense in terms of the Buddhist philosophy of mind, but it is the reason why mantras (sacred formulas) are efficacious,[5] and why study of a text such as Dogen's *Shobogenzo* ("the *Shobogenzo* is Dogen's own presence" to which "I must bring my whole self . . . in order to create my own esoteric act" [Kasulis 1985, p. 91]) or Tsong Khapas's *Essence of Pure Eloquence* can contribute to liberation from delusion. By imparting positive karma, even only that which is conceptual in nature, texts can undo the binding of negative karma, objective as well as conceptual. By reading mindfully, aware of these potential effects, and of the experience of emptiness that is provided by literary experience (reading and, even more, translation), these positive karmic effects are multiplied and deepened. Of course, negative karma can come from literary activity as well. But even this can be transmuted by a mindful reader/translator, just as "real" objective karma can be, through application of the proper conceptual or practical antidote.

Reading and rewriting, the "passing back and forth" of texts, is the "pure language" Benjamin spoke of, and it is an intimation of the sacred, synonymous with the "fathomless Reality" that "does not pass" but is always already everywhere. It is not gibberish, either, and notwithstanding Derrida, need not *necessarily* entail any precious subversion of rationalist "transparency." Indeed, to the extent that Derrida engages in difficulty for its own sake or as a display of virtuosity in language, like James Joyce in *Finnegan's Wake*, his are not fully texts at all by my definition, because they resist reading, and thereby enforce their own distance from a reader/rewriter's consciousness *to no purpose*. Texts of such chaste impenetrability reflect a concept of the true and the sacred as ineffable, inaccessible to consciousness, as essentially, purely *other*, and of all texts of "sacral" (ultimately true) import as gibberish. Such texts would reserve themselves, if not exclusively for the delectation of their author, then for a narrow circle of initiates, sworn to repeat the author's hermeticism. We need not fear the illusory transparency of the text, when we realize that texts do not exist apart from readings and (re)writings. Hermeticism then appears as a wasteful game of exclusion and self-aggrandizement, which attempts to betray the essence of free-flowing textuality, of the text as an extension of nature rather than a rejection of it.

Translation certainly does not have to occur on this level. Indeed, it usually does not. Most reading, for that matter, is done carelessly, within the category of nonascertaining cognition (when we see but do not notice, hear but do not listen to). Most scholarly readers and translators (readers who are also writers) give in to the tendency to reify some aspect or other of the text: either the object (these are bibliophiles), the mimetic "content" (treating it as though real, or as though having a direct connection to material phenomena, such as Marxists and historicists) or the formal (linguistic or semiotic) aspect of the text. None of these is "wrong," but neither do they fully realize the potential for realization implicit in the act of reading.

Then there is the question of motivation. Unless the correct motivation is present, neither reading nor translation will lead to *bodhi*, even though the reader reads and the translator writes in a way causing him or her to realize emptiness and the nonintegrity of self. But even then, there is no entropy; nothing is lost in the translation. As the poet James Merrill wrote, "Nothing's lost. Or else: all is translation/And every bit of us is lost in it/(Or found . . .)" (p. 10).

Part 2
Practice

4

Lafcadio Hearn, Decadence, and the Dream of Buddhist Japan

Although Chilupa travelled to Shambhala, it is sometimes described as like a pure land, a place beyond the reach of ordinary travel, a land that appears only to those of great merit.

—Jeffrey Hopkins
"History of the Kalachakra Tantra"

For in "his" Japan he found "his" Greece, where he sensed the ancient gods waiting to greet him at the end of his lifetime journey, when he arrived with his two pieces of luggage, on the other side of the world.

—Jonathan Cott
Wandering Ghost: the Odyssey of Lafcadio Hearn

This chapter is "practical" in two senses: it deals with someone whose literary pursuits led him to Buddhism; and my own procedure herein enacts the principles I have elaborated before, particularly in a reading of Hearn's translation of a story by Theophile Gautier, "La Morte Amoureuse" (literally, "The Loving Dead Woman," or "The Amorous Corpse"), which I take as an allegory of Hearn's own story. Hearn's translation of Gautier will, in its entirety, literally become part of this essay—of my translation of Hearn.

Lafcadio Hearn presents a case of someone who found, if not enlightenment, at least the path to enlightenment, through the language, literature, and culture of Buddhist Japan. His spiritual practice was literary—literature was for him a form of tantra long before he knew it—and it led him inexorably to Japan, and to Buddhism. His spiritual journey offers a chance to see how the theory of this book has worked, and might work again, in practice.

His spiritual/literary journey began with European predecadent literature, translations of the French writers Theophile Gautier and Pierre Loti, and ended with some of the most accurate and insightful representations of Japan and of Mahayana Buddhist thought that the West had yet seen, as well as with his conversion to Buddhism. The progress from decadence to Buddhism is not so surprising, either. Decadence, more even than deconstruction, revealed the cracks in the foundation of Western civilization, but could offer no cure for them. Buddhist thought was, at least for Hearn, a palliative if not a cure. To explain how will require both a brief recapitulation of Hearn's life prior to his conversion, as well as some discussion of the European decadence with which he identified as a young man.

Hearn was born on the island of Leucadia, off the Greek coast, to an Anglo-Irish father, Charles Hearn, a surgeon in the British Army, and Rosa Cassimati, a strange, beautiful, mercurial Greek mother of noble birth from the island. Hearn's parents were married for two years, though their first child, who died young, had been born out of wedlock. Lafcadio was christened in the Greek Orthodox Church, and did not come to Dublin with his mother until he was two years old, with gold earrings in his ears, long black hair, and dark skin. The Hearns thought he looked "Oriental." His father soon had the marriage annulled in Britain on the technicality that his illiterate Greek wife had not signed the papers. Rosa was away on a visit to her native islands when this occurred. Lafcadio was five years old, and never forgave his father.

After the annulment, he never saw his mother, and rarely ever saw his father, who was posted abroad for months at a time. He was reared by Sarah Brenane, a well-to-do great-aunt in Dublin who, alone of Charles Hearn's family, had accepted and befriended Lafcadio's mother, in a large old house full of dark corners and, according to Lafcadio, ghosts. The old lady was completely opposed to what she considered Patrick/Lafcadio's flights of fancy, and tried to cure the child's fear of the dark by locking him in his room at night with the lights out. He was rarely allowed to see his father or his father's new wife, or his younger brother James. His mother remarried, and returned only once to Ireland to see her sons, Patrick/Lafcadio and James, which the Hearn family refused to allow.

Patrick/Lafcadio's birth and childhood were characterized by scandal, displacement, and alienation. He had to give up the languages in which his mother first spoke to him, Italian and Romaic, in favor of English, which no matter how well he ever mastered it, never was in any sense his *mother tongue*. He grew up in a culture and a family from which he was made to feel fundamentally estranged, and never in his life gave up the sentiment that everything good in his person had come from his dark, absent, "Oriental" mother.

Lafcadio's escape before he escaped was through books. He quickly forgot the Romaic and Italian his mother had taught him, and outdid all his classmates in English composition. Any house as dark, gloomy, and large as his aunt's was bound to have a library, and hers did. This became the young Hearn's pleasure dome, his cabinet of artificial realities. Within it, he found squirreled away even a secret door that opened on his Greek beginnings:

> At last one day I discovered, in one unexplored corner of our library, several beautiful books about art—great folio books containing figures of gods and demigods, athletes and heroes, nymphs and fauns and nereids, and all the charming monsters—half-man, half-animal—of Greek mythology.
>
> How my heart leaped and fluttered on that happy day! Breathless I gazed; and the longer that I gazed the more unspeakably lovely those faces and forms appeared. Figure after figure dazzled, astounded, bewitched me. And this new delight was in itself a wonder—also a fear. *Something seemed to be thrilling out of those pictured pages—something invisible that made me afraid.* (my emphasis) (*Life and Letters*, I, p. 24)

Sarah Brenane's Catholic retainers were quick to discover her ward's pleasure and censor the pictures, excising breasts with a penknife and adding boxer shorts to the representations of male deities—an act that anticipated the role of the Church in the story by Théophile Gautier, "La Morte Amoureuse," that Hearn would appropriate by translation many years later. But it was already too late. He had glimpsed the very real power of books to create, or re-create a world in miniature, and through this realization he glimpsed the nature of reality as not distinct from mind, as something that could be shaped by words and thoughts—an insight shared with the hero of Gautier's story. In his aunt's library, Lafcadio escaped his gloomy environs, as Gautier's narrator/hero would escape the moribund existence of a priest in the arms of a supernatural, perhaps even imaginary woman, whose power was that of magical books, the power to bring imaginings to life.

After I had begun to know and love the elder gods, the world
again began to glow about me. Glooms that had brooded over it
slowly thinned away. The terror was not yet gone; but now I
wanted only reasons to disbelieve all that I had feared and hated.
In the sunshine, in the green of the fields, in the blue of the sky, I
found a gladness before unknown. Within myself new thoughts,
new imaginings, dim longings for I knew not what were quicken-
ing and thrilling. I looked for beauty, and everywhere found it in
passing faces—in attitudes and motions—in the poise of plants
and trees and—in long white clouds—in faint-blue lines of far-off
hills. At moments the simple pleasure of life would quicken to a
joy so large, so deep, that it frightened me. But at other times there
would come to me a new and strange sadness—a shadowy and
inexplicable pain. (*Life and Letters*, I, p. 28)

Lafcadio had discovered, in books, the power of the mind to make and
remake what is real.

This was the sort of precybernetic *virtual reality* that fascinated writers such as Theophile Gautier, Gustave Flaubert, and Joris-Karl Huysmans, some of whom Hearn would later translate. It has been supposed
by most critics and biographers that what drew Hearn to these "decadent" and pre-"decadent" writers was a certain lurid morbidity that he
shared with them, but I believe that there was a deeper affinity regarding
the latent force of words and the human mind to create artificial worlds.
This more than anything else is what defined the decadent aesthetic.

Hearn himself was a party to the Anglophone prejudice against
decadence as perversely overrefined, but he understood its affinities
with realism, which later literary historians would repress or ignore. In
his essay on "Decadence as Fine Art," Hearn wrote of "the enormous
and putrid mass of *realistic* rhyme and fiction which has been created
by the pessimistic philosophy and morbid feeling of certain French
writers" (my emphasis). He went on to associate decadence with the
empirical realism of Zola's school called naturalism, from which decadence directly sprang:

It appears that out of all the rotten rubbish of sensational naturalism and pessimism, *something false but singularly exquisite has been
evolved* [my emphasis] by the mental ferment of the time;—a theory has been crystallized,—an art-idea has been formed. It does
not really matter that the same theories should be accepted by

minds ever crawling and dwelling in nastiness, and by minds which soar so nearly to the sublime as to occasionally scorch their wings;—we may hope if not believe, that the former are only the larvae, the latter the perfect creatures. We cannot think that all the grubs will enjoy such metamorphosis; but if some do, we may dare to believe that the long mental decomposition of imaginative literature has not been utterly without a beneficial tendency.

The thin school of writers alluded to, seem to call themselves *decadents*, in dismal recognition of the intellectual era to which they belong; and they affect to worship only the crumbling, the effete, the ruined, the medieval, the Byzantine. So far, however, has this worship been carried that it finally brought about for them the evolution of a new form of that very thing from which they professed to be running away,—the Ideal.

Their confessed ambition is to carry the art of language to the supreme limit of expressive power,—to convey the most complete idea of an object with the utterance of an onomatopeia,—to paint a picture in a single line of text,—to make one quatrain frame in the whole beauty of a landscape, with color, form, shifting of light and shadow. In other words these realists have in their worship of *decadence* far exceeded the wildest dreams of Romanticism;—for it is not now the Ideal alone that they pursue, but the Absolutely Impossible. (*Essays*, pp. 28–30)

Hearn was closer to the truth in his assessment and understanding of decadent literature than virtually anyone has been since.

This is because he was a decadent writer himself, in every sense. His early penchant as a newspaper reporter for the lurid, the gory, and the macabre is impossible to overlook. This excerpt from a feature story he wrote for the Cincinnati *Enquirer* is exemplary.

[The Tallow District] is wholly deserted, darksome, desolate; and the stench which pervades its narrow streets suggests only the decay of death. You may walk upon the broken and filthy pavements for squares and squares without seeing any light but that of the street-lamps that gleam like yellow goblin-eyes, or hearing the footstep of a human being. The ghoulish grunting of hogs awaiting slaughter, the deep barking of ferocious tannery dogs, the snakish hissing of steam in rendering establishments, and the gurgling,

like a continuous death-rattle, of the black and poisonously foul
gutter streams alone break the deathly silence. To the right and
left nought is visible but tall broad fences or long frame buildings,
ghastly in the gleam of whitewash or gloomily black with the
grime of a smoky and greasy atmosphere. You can not cross the
road without befouling your shoe-leather frightfully. Your own
footsteps sound unpleasantly loud, and awake grim, hollow
echoes in all directions. The narrow streets and alleys are un-
evenly checkered by weirdly grotesque shadows, and inter-
esected by shadowy by-ways and deep doorways where murder-
ers might well hide. The deep howling of the dogs in the tannery
near by now excites frightful fancies. (Quoted in Cott, p. 40)

This was the real urban nightmare of the Industrialized West that inspired Baudelaire's *Flowers of Evil*. In his first stint as a journalist in Cincinnati, Hearn made his reputation with a graphic account of a violent
murder case, "The Tanyard Murder" ("Gurgling Noise of the Stran-
gling Man"; "The Hideous Mass of Reeking Cenders"; "The Grinning
Teeth Shone Ghastly White"), and became known for stories such as
one in which he exposed the cruelties of the slaughterhouse with a vividness still hard to bear today, translating into words for his readers'
delectation the taste of a glass of blood from a freshly killed cow, and
another in which he visited the shop of a man whose livelihood was to
assemble skeletons from putrid remains, assisted by his two angelic
children, George and Katie, aged eleven and nine. So Lafcadio's deri-
sive remarks about the subject matter of some decadent writers might
just as well have applied to his own.

      Though like the best decadent writers, like Baudelaire, he be-
lieved also in the power of words, of writing, to remake the world, in
words as a door to "the Absolutely Impossible." In Theravada Buddhism, meditation in the filth and reek of the cremation ground is part
of any practitioner's progress; what must be learned there is the illusion of the body's integrity—the same thematic that infuses so many of
Baudelaire's poems in which the lover disintegrates into a rotted
corpse; in Vajrayana, or Tantric Buddhism, the charnel ground meditation goes beyond the realization of the body's limitations, to cultivate
the mind's power to transmute horror into bliss—to make flowers of
evil, as Baudelaire did with his poems. Hearn would only find his way
out of decadence through Buddhism, but it would also be correct to say
that he only found his way to Buddhism through decadence.

•

To understand why and how this should be so, we must first understand that "decadence," mostly French but with practitioners also in England and Italy, is really inappropriately named, even though Hearn and many so-called decadents delighted in the misnomer. From the Latin *de-cadere*, meaning to fall away, the word implies a decline in moral values, literary values, or both that is not very often justified. The implication alone has meant that "decadent" literature has been relegated to a marginal and suspect status within the Western canon, even while many writers such as Richard Gilman have pointed out how arbitrary the term is and how little it contributes to any understanding of the literary works it is supposed to describe. The persistence of the term, with all its vaguely negative connotations, has blinded us for a century to the importance of the literary movement it (mis)names. This is unfortunate because, in the literature we have called "decadent," the roots of many preoccupations and insecurities that have structured our contemporary culture are to be found, from deconstruction to virtual reality, not to mention the beginnings of Lafcadio Hearn's "enlightenment."

Though he had many antecedents, the first genuine decadent was J.-K. Huysmans, author of the novel *Against the Grain*, published in 1883, which was to become a kind of decadent manifesto. Joris-Karl (Charles Marie Georges) Huysmans first became known as a disciple of Emile Zola, and thus as an adherent of naturalism—that school of literary practice founded on the premise that literature could, and should precisely imitate the scientific and cyclical patterns of nature. In practice naturalism required a rather journalistic, laboriously detailed prose narrative that omitted nothing in the name of good taste (hence contemporary descriptions of Zola's work as "pornography," although by today's standards it seems quite politely discreet). Hearn wrote of naturalism:

> The probabilities are that Zola and his school,—despite the intense brutality of their first recoil from Romanticism, and despite all the abominations for which the Naturalistic philosophy offered so miserable an excuse,—have really laid the foundations of a magnificent art which will only be developed after them, but which will surpass the best of what was done before them. They have unconsciously revealed to the world the secret of a New Idealism. (*Essays*, p. 124)

In 1877 Huysmans published *Emile Zola et l'Assommoir*, in which he set forth his allegiance to Zola and naturalism for all to see. The publication of *A Rebours* is usually thought to represent a break with the realistic practice of naturalism, and with Zola. It certainly did coincide with a rift between the two writers, as Huysmans himself admitted in his preface to the 1902 edition of the novel, but how and to what extent *A Rebours* broke with realism and with the literary past is a more difficult question. It certainly is true that *A Rebours* became, almost instantly, the manifesto of a new literary school with which such writers as Comte Philippe Auguste Mathias de Villiers de l'Isle-Adam, Jules Laforgue, Tristan Corbière, and even the great poet Mallarmé would become associated. The term *décadence* had been used by Paul Bourget not long before the publication of *A Rebours* in a study of Baudelaire, *Théorie de la décadence*, and *A Rebours* coincided with Huysmans' return to the darker, more explicitly Baudelairean or "charnel ground" side of himself apparent in his earliest published work. In appropriating the term to describe the protagonist of *A Rebours*, Des Esseintes, Huysmans changed the history of French letters. The novel itself would become, as the cliché goes, as great a milestone for the end of the century as Chateaubriand's *Le Génie du Christianisme* had been for its beginning. Des Esseintes became a sort of fictional cult hero for a whole generation of young would-be literati and was memorialized by Mallarmé in the poem "Prose pour Des Esseintes."

But *A Rebours* might also be considered a manifesto of realism, of a *return* to realism as understood by Flaubert before Zola—Flaubert, whose most extravagant, fantastical, and evidently predecadent novel, *The Temptation of Saint Anthony*, would be translated by none other than Lafcadio Hearn. *A Rebours* is in fact as much a logical development of the "realistic," laconically descriptive style thought by many to have reached its zenith in Flaubert, as it is a renunciation of Zola's naturalism. As surely as the word comes from the Latin *de-cadere*, "to fall from," a fall is implied, but one that in fact began with earlier writers such as Flaubert.

The object of Flaubert's realism is not the same as Zola's. The 'real' for Flaubert is rather our perception of the real than anything that may exist apart from or prior to perception. This concept of reality echoes that of Buddhist epistemology, as well as that of the German philosopher Schopenhauer, whose pessimism influenced Huysmans profoundly. Schopenhauer, the first Western philosopher to be influenced by Buddhist thought, is responsible for a great many common Western misapprehensions of Buddhism (for instance, that Buddhism is essentially pessimistic, nihilistic, and ascetic). But this is not all Schopenhauer's fault; Buddhism was very poorly understood in the West during his life. And on this point—the phenomenal, rather than noumenal nature of reality—he was quite in harmony with genuine Buddhism, and so were Flaubert and Huysmans.

Only when Huysmans' debt to Flaubertian realism is understood can the extent of his "innovation" in *A Rebours* be properly addressed. *A Rebours* and its hero, Des Esseintes, pursue with relentless rigor the logic of realism as literary special effects, the manipulation of the reader's senses and desire through language in an effort to sustain momentarily the "hallucination" that there is no difference between the text and the real, no difference between the fiction being recounted, or imagination, and actual events. Des Esseintes withdraws from the world and seals himself off from it in an effort to attain perfect control over his reality and to reduce to nothing, within the walls of his house, the difference between imagination and reality, artifice and nature. He attempts in effect to create the illusion of various realities in order to modulate his own sensations.

> Sometimes, in the afternoon, when by chance Des Esseintes was awake and upright, he would maneuver the set of pipes and conduits that emptied the aquarium and refilled it with pure water, and introduced drops of colored essences, obtaining thus, in his own peculiar way, the green or briny, opaline or silvery tones of real rivers which vary according to the color of the sky, the intensity of the sunlight, the more or less accentuated threats of rain, according, in a word, to the state of the season and the atmosphere.

> He imagined himself thus on the between-deck of a brig, and curiously he contemplated marvelous mechanical fishes, mounted like pieces of clockwork, which passed before the glass of the porthole and caught on synthetic grasses; or while breathing the smell of tar that had been blown into the room before he entered, he examined, hung up on the wall, colored engravings like the ones at steamboat agencies and at Lloyd's, of steamers on their way to Valparaiso and la Plata, and framed paintings on which were inscribed the itineraries of the Royal mail steam packet line, of the Lopez and Valéry companies, the freights and the ports of postal services of the Atlantic.

Then, when he was weary of consulting these guides, he would rest his gaze by looking at chronometers and compasses, sextants and calipers, binoculars and maps scattered on a table above which stood a single book, bound in marine calfskin, the adventures of Arthur Gordon Pym, specially printed for him, on laid paper, pure grained, each sheet selected by hand, with a sea-gull watermark.

Finally he could see fishing poles, nets burnished to a tan color, rolls of reddish sails, a minuscule anchor made of cork, painted black, thrown all in a heap next to the door which led to the kitchen through a padded hallway that absorbed all odors and sounds, just as did the corridor joining the dining room and the study.

He procured for himself thus, without moving at all, the rapid, almost instantaneous sensations of a lengthy voyage, and that pleasure of displacement which, in fact, exists only in memory and almost never in the present, in the same moment in which it is executed; he imbibed fully, at leisure, without fatigue, without turmoil, in that compartment whose contrived disorder, transitory appearance and temporary installation corresponded precisely to the brief time he spent there, to the limited time of his meals, and contrasted absolutely with his study, a definitive room, neat, well established, outfitted for the good maintenance of a domestic existence. (pp. 78–79; my translation, as are all to follow, from *A Rebours*).

In Des Esseintes's house, reality is subordinate to books, to the imagination, rather than the other way around. How better to meditate on emptiness? But Des Esseintes never goes beyond emptiness as mere vacuity.

The same effort in Flaubert is nowhere more clearly elaborated than in his *Trois Contes (Three Tales)*. The unity of the *Trois Contes* is tellingly grounded in the representation of three kinds of religious experience. In the naïveté of the first story's main character, Félicité, there is no difference between the text of the Bible and reality, between a map and the terrain it represents, between a parrot and God—the real and its representation are one in her ecstatic, hallucinatory simplemindedness. In the second story, another animal—the stag, which speaks a prophecy to the protagonist—becomes the same sort of figure as the parrot, representing the way in which the mute, objectively real depends on language, on representation, on human perception, to embody and to become what we understand as real. His encounter with the stag causes the main character, Julien, to suffer a kind of madness of uncertainty. He is no longer sure of the difference between the real and the text (of the real), between bloodlust (material desire) and another, spiritual, *script*-ural desire. This discrepancy is collapsed in his final hallucinatory experience of God. Similarly, in the third and final story, *Hérodias*, Herod's erotic, material desire is contrasted with the scriptural, religious desire of John the Baptist. Salomé, the object of Herod's purely material desire, is mute movement; the Baptist is nothing but a voice crying in the wilderness, housed like the stag's and the parrot's voices in a "brutish" body: "I shall cry out like a bear, like a wild ass . . ." (Flaubert II, p. 665). The reality, the desirability, of both Salomé and the Baptist is a matter of the way they are perceived. The contrast at the end between the Baptist's head as, on the one hand, just one item among the detritus of the night's festivities, and on the other, a religious talisman, is one more representation of this paradox.

The hero of Huysmans' *A Rebours*, Des Esseintes, must be read as the figure of an individual who has determined to live his life by the same precepts and logic that govern Flaubert's fiction. Des Esseintes means to control and willfully to manipulate his own sensations with such care and precision as to create a "real fiction" so enveloping that it leaves no room for contamination by any exterior, alien, and uncontrolled reality. He has a preference for Latin authors because their language is "dead":

> The interest that Des Esseintes brought to the Latin language did not diminish now that, completely rotten, it hung, losing its members, oozing pus, retaining only with difficulty, in all the corruption of its body, a few firm parts that Christians would detach in order to marinate in the brine of their new language. (p. 91)

Not only does he duplicate the smells and decor of travel in his house, but he has a "mouth organ" *(orgue à bouche)*, a collection of liquors of various tastes correlated to approximate a degustatory music:

> Des Esseintes would drink a drop here and there, playing interior symphonies on himself; succeeded in obtaining, in the throat, sensations analogous to those that music poured into the ear. . . . each liqueur corresponded, according to him, to the sound of an instrument. Dry curaçao, for instance, to the clarinet. (p. 99)

Sometimes he transposed or "duplicated," by taste, an already existing musical composition, and sometimes he "composed melodies himself" (p. 100). In a word, "artifice seemed to Des Esseintes the distinctive mark of human genius" (p. 80). He is said to believe it possible "to satisfy desires reputed to be the most difficult to please in everyday life by a light subterfuge, by an approximative sophistication of [surrogate for] the object pursued by those very desires" (p. 79). He lives by the rule and practice of *adroit mensonge,* adroit lying.

He keeps a pet cricket rather than a parrot, which, however, plays the same role as Félicité's parrot Loulou in the first of Flaubert's *Trois Contes:* just as the bird served to manipulate Félicité's experience of the real, subsuming all sorts of meanings such as her nephew's whereabouts, the Holy Spirit, and the New World, Des Esseintes's cricket serves to manipulate his perceptions, memories, emotions, sensations. The difference is that Des Esseintes knows very well that he is being manipulated, is in fact manipulating himself. He is as sophisticated and subtle a "reader" as one could wish for, unlike the naive Félicité. This, indeed, is the governing principle behind his careful orchestration of all the physical sensations to which he is subject, all of his surroundings. That manipulation of the reader (Des Esseintes) by the author (Des Esseintes) or the author's words, which occurs here within the text (in Des Esseintes's effort to create a "real fiction"), perfectly duplicates Flaubert's project as a realist: to create a literary reality more credible, more immediate than phenomenal reality, to manipulate the reader's imagination so adroitly as to collapse the gap between the text and the real. Des Esseintes is a realist even more zealous than Flaubert: he practices *in his life* the Flaubertian principle of allusion to at least three of the senses in a descriptive passage of writing in order to seduce the reader's imagination into suspending incredulity. Des Esseintes's pet cricket is the figure of a logic implicit in the parrot Loulou, in the stag that prophesies to Julien, in the head of John the Baptist and the dance of Salomé, but the cricket is more explicitly a figure for *self-conscious* Flaubertian realistic style, the manipulation of imaginary sensation. While he "hallucinates" in the cricket's voice all sorts of meanings that are not there, precisely as Félicité did with the parrot, he knows perfectly well what he is doing:

> Thus, out of hatred, out of scorn for his childhood, he had hung from the ceiling of this room a little cage of silver wire in which an imprisoned cricket sang, as they had [in his childhood] in the ashes

of the fireplaces of the castle of Lourps; when he would hear this sound, heard so many times before, all the constrained and mute evenings at his mother's, all the abdication of a suffering and repressed youth rose up before him, and then, in the thrashings of the woman whom he was caressing mechanically and whose words or whose laugh broke his vision and brought him brusquely back to reality, in the bedroom, on the ground, a tumult would rise up in his soul, a need of vengeance for the sorrows endured, a raging desire to soil by turpitude these familial memories, a furious desire to pant on cushions of flesh, to exhaust to their last drops the most vehement and the most bitter of carnal excesses. (pp. 69–70)

Both Huysmans, in *A Rebours*, and Flaubert are ultimately phenomenal, rather than empirical realists like Zola. They believe, unlike Zola, that the real does not exist apart from our perception of it. If we can manipulate our own perceptions, we can manipulate our reality. Huysmans goes one step further in showing how the principles of realistic style, and the implications of Flaubertian realism, apply not just to literature but to life, to our real perception of the real. Decadence, then, must be a *return* to Flaubert's (and Schopenhauer's) view of reality, and a departure from Zola's pseudo-scientific literary empiricism. In the fictional character of Des Esseintes it becomes more evident than ever that the theoretical implications of realism, and the realistic implications of theory, are decadent —that is to say, antirealistic, or as Lafcadio Hearn would insist, *idealistic*. Perhaps it would make more sense to say that decadence is nothing but the theoretical development of mimetic realism to its logical end. This may be the best answer to the question of what decadence is.

The idea of constructing artificial realities in miniature, of, for instance, replicating London in one's home, is an old one in Asia, harkening back to the subject of the first chapter of this book: bonsai and penjing, miniature trees and landscapes. Des Esseintes's precursor was a Daoist or Buddhist hermit/shaman. "Whenever hermits draw or cultivate dwarf plants in a miniature landscape," wrote Rolf Stein, "they create for themselves, as does a magician-illusionist, a *separate world in miniature*" (p. 52). In the view of Daoism and hermetic Buddhism, not only trees but anything "old" and "no longer used," such as Latin, becomes "*ling* [full of spiritual power]."

In China, any old object, animate or inanimate, can rise to the ranks of the spirits as it grows older . . . All these things share the nature of *ku-ching*, "old essences." . . . A *ku-shu* (old tree) is also the term for a twisted, strange, dwarf tree growing in a miniature garden . . . To cultivate such a miniature garden in one's own home brings longevity and the shining, firm skin of one in the full vigor of maturity. (pp. 96–97)

Also just as important in Eastern mysticism as it was in European decadence is the concept of enclosedness, of withdrawal from the world:

Just as animals, stones, and plants do not achieve the complete blossoming of their remarkable properties unless they live withdrawn in the depths of mountains and forests, humans cannot hope to reach the fullness of their vital power, to reach purity and integrity—that is, the inviolability of their purest nature—unless they live hidden in a retreat closed to the outside world. . . .

Imitating the withdrawal of animals, stones, and plants, people create a miniature enclosed site, perfect and complete in its inviolate nature, within the surrounding wall of dwellings and, for even stronger reasons, in hermitages . . . In the courtyard and behind the screen stands a little container garden. . . .

To achieve or to regain immortality, Taoists go into hiding *(tsang)* in the mountains, collecting herbs and precious woods. In order to do this, *they do not have to leave their own home.* (my emphasis) (Stein, p. 109)

In Des Esseintes's case, it is precious *words* not woods, that are collected, but the idea is the same. The container landscape does not simply represent, but *is* the whole of living nature in microcosm; the habitation of the Daoist/Buddhist hermit embodies the same idea, which is not just an aesthetic principle: the whole universe in a small, enclosed space. What is for Des Esseintes the means of a rich, but empty aestheticism, is in the context of Asian thought the access to spiritual realization and reconciliation with nature, not alienation from it.

Des Esseintes's quest lacks any grounding beyond pure, Cartesian aestheticism, and so it ends up making him ill. For his author, Huysmans, decadence was a circular detour that led to a place more ancient than the one where he began, but in the same historical stream—to an extreme Catholicism, another expression of Western materialism. But in spite of its abortive immediate result, Huysmans' aestheticism pointed toward literary experience as analogous in spiritual purpose to the penjing and bonsai of the East.

Edgar Allan Poe's life and work might also be said to loosely parallel the fictional trajectory of Des Esseintes. Poe—much admired by Hearn, as well as by the fictional Des Esseintes—entered the French canon through the translations of Mallarmé and Baudelaire, and his paradoxical insistence on the mechanical nature of literature feeds directly into the idea, already suggested by Flaubert and Huysmans, of literature as a machine that produces the real, and of the real as a "mechanical" process of self-generation involving all sorts of essentially literary techniques.[1] The notion of the machine as a metaphor for literature and for reality, and so for the discontinuity and contingency of art and the real, would be developed by Alfred Jarry to the point that machine and literary trope are figures for each other as part of a process of production that only ever produces more production, further substitutions. A Marxist might say that the realist/decadent text "produces" the reality of capitalist consumerism. And it would not be wrong to say so.

Ulimately such a literary machine must subsume and deconstruct the author-ity of an inherently real reading and writing subjectivity, and this is what happens in the poetry of Arthur Rimbaud, or in Lautréamont's *Les Chants de Maldoror (The Songs [or Cantos] of Maldoror)*: the distinction between author and text, and between textual content and the reader's affective response to the text, are reduced as much as possible. *Maldoror*, like Hearn's journalistic pieces, is a violent text that elicits visceral responses from a reader. Inasmuch as his text produces more violent responses—of revulsion, moral indignation, or morbid fascination—in the reader than *Madame Bovary*, Lautréamont might claim to be a more accomplished realist than Flaubert. He succeeds in forcing the text and the reader's experience, the reader's intellectual and affective "reality," to coincide. What occurred on the pages of Huysmans' text—the conflation in Des Esseintes of writer, reader and character—is carried one step further, to engulf the actual reader in the illusory "reality" of the text. It is "Maldoror," Lautréamont's text—*and* authorial persona—who is the cricket here, and we who are in the place of Des Esseintes: "Have you not noticed the gracility of a pretty cricket, of sprightly movements, in the sewers of Paris? There is only that one there: it was Maldoror!" (p. 232).

The same conflation of text and reality occurred in the life of Lafcadio Hearn, who wrote himself. He was always the protagonist of all his literary production: he found in Japan the place of his imaginings,

and in Buddhist thought the way out of his aunt's library, out of the circular solipsism of Western literary production (decadence), out of his
own personal literary journey that began with the artificial reality of a
book on Greek mythology.

   Why Japan? Why specifically *Japanese* Buddhism? In nineteenth-
century Europe, fascination with Japan was closely associated with the
taste for artificial realities long before Hearn arrived on the shores of
Nihon. Late-nineteenth-century Parisian art critics such as Zacharie
Astruc and Philippe Burty wrote a great deal about this affinity; Burty
is thought to have been the first to use the term "Japonisme" in 1872 to
describe the work of artists like Degas, Pissarro, Bracquemond, and
Manet, influenced by the art of Japan. The phenomenon of Japonisme,
said to have begun with Felix Bracquemond's discovery of an album of
woodblock prints by Hokusai at a printer's shop in Paris in 1856, was
much stimulated and fortified by the Paris Universal Expositions in
1867 and 1878. It was significant enough to warrant sneering dismissal
by Champfleury in his article of 1868, "La Mode des Japoniaiseries"
("The Fashion of Japanitwittery"). Several Japanophiles, including
Bracquemond, Burty, and Astruc, founded the "Société du Jing-lar" or
Jing-lar Society, in the 1860s, and would meet regularly to indulge a
common obsession with Japanese food, culture, and art—to play at
being in what they imagined was the Japanese manner. This sonnet
commemorates the group:

> The Jinglar is a liqueur
> To be skimmed from bronzes;
> It exalts, in Paris, the heart
> And the precious art of eight bonzes [Buddhist monks].
>
> The Buddhas, beneath giant pines,
> In the flowers of the magic lotus,
> Adored it—their gaping gazes
> To fill with a lethargic dream.
>
> Hail! wine of mysterious ones
> By you are our deliriums illumined
> Master of brushes and of lyres.
>
> You come from glorious Japan
> Evoking new customs

To be sung by wise men.
(Weisberg, p. 18; my translation)

The influence on European art would grow; van Gogh copied several Hiroshige prints in oil, and the impact on the work of Monet, Renoir, Gauguin, Toulouse-Lautrec, and countless others is obvious as well as amply documented. Theodore Duret, an early pro-impressionist critic, wrote in his preface to *Works in Oil and Pastel by the Impressionists of Paris* (1886):

> Well it may seem strange to say it, but it is none the less true, that before the arrival among us of the Japanese picture books, there was no one in France who dared to seat himself on the banks of a river and to put side by side on his canvas, a roof frankly red, a white-washed wall, a green poplar, a yellow road, and blue water. (Weisberg, p. 118)

Pissarro wrote in a letter to his son that "Hiroshige [the great Japanese woodblock print artist] is a marvellous impressionist" (Weisberg, pp. 188–89). Edward Morse added that

> What the Japanese were able to do with their primitive methods of block-printing and a few colors, required the highest genius of our artists and chromo-lithographers; and even then the subtle spirit which the artist sought for could not be caught. (p. xxix)

And Kenicha Yoshida dismisses the matter of influence altogether:

> Japanese painting may have influenced the Impressionists, and Impressionism in its turn may have been appropriated by Japanese painters; there does not seem to be anything extraordinary about this, since it is not schools that matter but artistic perception, which is the common property of artists. (p. 23)

Colta Ives's *Great Wave: The Influence of Japanese Woodcuts on French Prints*, and *Japonisme: Japanese Influence on French Art 1854–1910* by Weisberg and others, document the phenomenon in great detail, including the fact that virtually no French or American Japanophiles had ever been near Japan (which thus, because it was unknown and inaccessible, came to represent the artificial or imaginary realm *par excellence*), and yet they indulged in an obsessive mania for things Japanese that was to have a profound impact on the evolution of Western art. Neither painter James McNeill Whistler nor critic Zacharie Astruc had any personal experience of Japan when they nearly came to fisticuffs over a choice Japanese bibelot.

Probably none of this constitutes a real answer to the question, "Why Japan?" It merely reformulates the particular question as a general statement.

Hearn's Japan was, much like that of Whistler and Astruc, always, from the first day he set foot there, a kind of faerie, in the sense in which the *OED* defines that term: "beautiful and unsubstantial, visionary, unreal."

> Elfish everything seems; for everything as well as everybody is small, and queer, and mysterious [like Hearn himself, who was five foot three inches tall, and nearly blind, described by his first editor, John Cockerill, as a "distorted brownie . . . uncanny and indescribable"]: the little houses under their blue roofs, the little shop-fronts hung with blue, and the smiling little people in their blue costumes. The illusion is only broken by the occasional passing of a tall foreigner, and by divers shop-signs bearing announcements in absurd attempts at English. Nevertheless such discords only serve to emphasize reality; they never materially lessen the fascination of the funny little streets. ("My First Day in the Orient," *Glimpses*, pp. 2–3)

Many years later, the French critic Roland Barthes would write of Japan: "The unknown language" that comprises not only words but gestures, clothing, decoration, ". . . forms around me . . . a faint vertigo, sweeping me into its artificial emptiness, which is consummated only for me: I live in the interstice, delivered from any fulfilled meaning" (p. 9). For Hearn, as for Barthes, the "elfishness" was not so much a matter of size as of *signs*:

> And finally, while you are still puzzling over the mystery of things, there will come to you like a revelation the knowledge that most of the amazing picturesqueness of these streets is simply due to the profusion of Chinese and Japanese characters in white, black, blue, or gold, decorating everything,—even surfaces of

doorposts and paper screens. Perhaps, then, for one moment, you will imagine the effect of English lettering substituted for those magical characters; and the mere idea will give to whatever aesthetic sentiment you may possess a brutal shock. (*Glimpses*, p. 4)

This writing was not only in a language Hearn did not know, but resembled in no way the writing of any language he did know, allowing him to suppose that "An ideograph does not make upon the Japanese brain any impression similar to that created in the Occidental brain by a letter or combination of letters." The impression he was talking about, however, was the one that occurred in his own very Occidental brain.[2] Because it was so strange to him, and perfectly opaque, yet beautiful, this writing was able to become for Hearn a palpable, living atmosphere of pure, floating signifiers, in which the usual economy of signs, according to which things always mean something other than themselves, was exploded or transcended or rendered moot by a sense of perfect immediacy and presence, by a *satori* in which he read and felt (like Barthes later, but apparently more intensely) the beautiful emptiness of all words and all things, and imagined it to be a unique quality of Japanese streets.

And if this was true, Japan had to be the goal of all European decadence, as Hearn himself had defined it—Hearn's decadence was above all a matter of words, of the magic word or words that would unite the human with the "unknowable":

The extravagance of supposing that all human ideas, sensations, desires can be eventually compressed into one word, the utterance of which shall suffice to annihilate man, or at last to blend him forever with the Unknowable, may certainly be ridiculed as a tenet in this serious nineteenth century; but there is poetry in the fancy, as well as a pseudo-philosophy immemorially old. For thousands of years,—perhaps for thousands of ages,—men have been seeking after this ideal of expression, just as they have pursued the delusions of alchemy, believed in the lies of astrology, hunted for the jewel in the toad's head, and the dragon-stone, and the self-luminous carbuncle. Various faiths aided the search; the Brahmins claimed to know the mystic Word, whose utterance elevated men to heaven;—the Buddhists held that the syllable OM gave power to enter Nirvana to those who knew its deeper signification;—in the Kabbala we read of the Name by the combinations

of whose letters men may be created from dust;—in the Talmud
we are told of the Ineffable Appellation of forty-two letters, revealed only to those beloved of the Lord;—nor is it necessary to
cite the magical attributes which Islamic fancy lends to the name
of Allah, engraved upon emeralds, or upon seals, or written upon
the million charms sold by the marabouts of the Maghreb. . . .
Thus it would seem that the extremes touched by pessimism have
given out a force of repulsion which is hurling minds back even
beyond the point started from,—beyond all conceivable idealism,—beyond all rational imagination,—beyond the limits of the
world itself into the mysteries of Time and Space and Infinitude!
("Decadence as an Art," *Essays*, pp. 32–33)[3]

In the *language* of Japanese being, the mundane and the supramundane
seemed to Hearn, as to Barthes more than half a century later, to form a
unity.

It is not surprising, indeed, considering the strangely personal,
animate, esoteric aspect of Japanese lettering, that there should be
such wonderful legends of calligraphy, relating how words written by holy experts became incarnate, and descended from their
tablets to hold converse with mankind. (*Glimpses*, p. 5)

So that the very language, the Japanese way of being, the place, became
an object of passionate desire.

•

We should believe that passion, though buried again and again, can neither die nor rest. Those who have vainly loved only seem to die; they
really live on in generations of hearts, that their desire may be fulfilled.
They wait, perhaps through centuries, for the reincarnation of shapes beloved,—forever weaving into the dreams of youth their vapory compos-
ite of memories. Hence the ideals unattainable,—the haunting of troubled souls by the Woman-never-to-be-known.

—Lafcadio Hearn
"By Force of Karma"

For the living present, I reflected, is the whole dead past.

—Lafcadio Hearn
"A Serenade"

A floating world: this is the meaning of *ukiyo*, which in the term *ukiyo-e*, pictures of the floating world, refers to the color woodblock prints for which the Japanese have been famous since the country was reopened to the West, and which wielded such a profound influence on Western artists from Toulouse-Lautrec to van Gogh. "Here are [the woodblock artist] Hokusai's own figures," wrote Hearn, "walking about in straw rain-coats, and immense mushroom-shaped hats of straw" (*Glimpses*, p. 10). The Japanese word *(ukiyo-e)* refers to the Buddhist concept of this world as an illusion, the world of vanity and impermanence, and traditionally the prints depicted denizens of the Japanese *demimonde*, actors, and courtesans. Something about these haunting images, from which the third dimension is deliberately banished, even when there is linear perspective, allies them to the "floating signifiers" of Hearn's first day in Japan. There is something "elfish," dreamlike, about them, and yet Japan has long seen something essential about itself mirrored in them, and we believe we see that essence revealed. An essence that is Japanese, of course, but also living in the depths of ourselves.

A ghost, perhaps; the sheer shape of something nameless that haunts our thoughts, waking and sleeping, and our words. Is that the idea of Japan? In Hearn's own words, "a *strangeness* of beauty like the musical thought of a vanished time" ("A Serenade," *Exotics and Retrospectives*, p. 243)? The more familiar, bucolic scenes of Hokusai and Hiroshige notwithstanding, ghosts have always been a favorite subject of the woodblock artists in Japan, never more so than in Hearn's day. In "The Eternal Haunter" (part of *Exotics and Retrospectives*, 1898), he noted: "This year the Tokyo color-prints—*Nishiki-e* [literally, "brocade" prints, meaning that they used colored pigments]—seem to me of unusual interest." Not just for their technical and artistic excellence, but on account of supernatural subject matter.

> My latest purchase has been a set of weird studies,—spectres of all kinds known to the Far East, including many varieties not yet discovered in the West. Some are extremely unpleasant; but a few are really charming . . . Can you guess what [this one] represents? . . . Yes, a girl,—but what kind of a girl? Study it a little. . . . Very lovely, is she not, with that shy sweetness in her downcast gaze,— that light and dainty grace, as of a resting butterfly? . . . No, she is not some Psyche of the most Eastern East, in the sense that you mean—but she is a soul. Observe that the cherry-flowers falling

from the branch above, are passing *through* her form. See also the folds of her robe, below, melting into blue faint mist. How delicate and vapory the whole thing is! It gives you the feeling of spring; and all those fairy colors are the colors of a Japanese spring-morning.

. . . No, she is not the personification of any season. Rather she is a dream—such a dream as might haunt the slumbers of Far-Eastern youth. (pp. 293–94)

It is an ancient commonplace in Chinese and Japanese folklore that trees and flowers have spirits that may appear in human form. The print Hearn was describing depicted a cherry-tree spirit. "Only in the twilight of morning or evening she appears, gliding about her tree;—and whoever sees her must love her. . . . There is a legend of one tree-spirit who loved a man, and even gave him a son; but such conduct was quite at variance with the shy habits of her race." Hearn insists that "to me this Japanese dream is true,—true, at least, as human love is. Considered even as a ghost it is true." What if we consider it as the ghost of Japan itself, the idea of Japan? For Hearn, all such ectoplasmic visions are archetypes of desire. "The eternal haunter" is the spectral outline of everything one ever could fail to have, or fear to lose, the perfect shape of perfectly requited desire, and "her tree is the measure-less, timeless, billion-branching Tree of Life,—even the World-Tree, Yggdrasil, whose roots are in Night and Death, whose head is above the Gods."

That Japan was above all, for Hearn *ghostly* is evident in the names of books he published about his adopted country: *In Ghostly Japan*, *Kwaidan* ("Weird Tales"), "In the Cave of the Children's Ghosts," "Of Souls," "Of Ghosts and Goblins," "The Literature of the Dead," "Of Moon-Desire," and so forth. Hearn delighted in listening to his Japanese wife recount the traditional ghost stories of her country. I have already alluded to Hearn's translation of a Western, predecadent "ghost story" by Théophile Gautier, "La Morte Amoureuse," which translates literally as "The Amorous Dead Woman" (Hearn called his version simply "Clarimonde," the name of the story's subject). I propose that this story contains an allegory of Hearn's love affair with Japan and his escape from the impasse of Western materialism through Japanese Buddhism. Such a reading has never been proposed by any biographer or critic of Hearn's work before, but there is circumstantial evidence that

Hearn himself would not disagree with it. The female protagonist of Gautier/Hearn's story is a figure embodying all of the ghostly yet palpable allures of Japan for Hearn, and yet Hearn's story, happily, ended differently from the one he translated. The story is short enough, and Hearn dead long enough (the copyright long expired), that I am able to reproduce it here. It is interlarded with excerpts from Hearn's writings on Japan and my own commentary. Here, then, is the theory elaborated in the first part of this book, translated into practice: Hearn's text is not distinct from Gautier's, and mine is not distinct from either. By Hearn I mean nothing simple, but an amalgam of all the different texts that comprised the writer/translator: Lafcadio/Patrick the Greek/Irish boy, the American journalist, and the Buddhist/naturalized Japanese, along with all the texts he had read and translated (Gautier, for instance), and all the readers who have read and translated (figuratively and literally) him, including me.

The story's plot is simple. A young priest is seduced by a beautiful vampire, with whom he has an idyllic affair. She takes from him only the small amount of blood necessary to sustain her existence. Far from the usual representation of a vampire in Western literature, Clarimonde is the perfect lover. It is hard for the priest to know if his life with her is dreamed, but it comes to seem more real than his other existence in the Church. Meanwhile the Church, in the person of an older priest, rails at the "evil" represented by the vampire Clarimonde. That evil is nothing but a world in which the pleasures of the flesh are not subject to moral censure, and the binarisms of Western philosophy and theology have no hold. Such a world was Japan at the end of the last century, when Lafcadio Hearn arrived there.

The story begins with the young priest, who has grown old now, responding to a question: Has he ever loved? His reply, intended as a warning against love, resounds ironically as a wistful grief for its loss.

BROTHER, YOU ask me if I have ever loved. Yes. My story is a strange and terrible one; and though I am sixty-six years of age, I scarcely dare even now to disturb the ashes of that memory. To you I can refuse nothing; but I should not relate such a tale to any less experienced mind. So strange were the circumstances of my story, that I can scarcely believe myself to have ever actually been a party to them. For more than three years I remained the victim of a most singular and diabolical illusion. Poor country priest though I was, I led every night in a dream—would to God it had been all a dream!—a most worldly life, a damning life, a life of

Sardanapalus. One single look too freely cast upon a woman well nigh caused me to lose my soul; but finally by the grace of God and the assistance of my patron saint, I succeeded in casting out the evil spirit that possessed me. My daily life was long interwoven with a nocturnal life of a totally different character. By day I was a priest of the Lord, occupied with prayer and sacred things; by night, from the instant that I closed my eyes I became a young nobleman, a fine connoisseur in women, dogs, and horses; gambling, drinking, and blaspheming, and when I awoke at early daybreak, it seemed to me, on the other hand, that I had been sleeping, and had only dreamed that I was a priest. Of this somnambulistic life there now remains to me only the recollection of certain scenes and words which I cannot banish from my memory; but although I never actually left the walls of my presbytery, one would think to hear me speak that I were a man who, weary of all worldly pleasures, had become a religious, seeking to end a tempestuous life in the service of God, rather than an humble seminarist who has grown old in this obscure curacy, situated in the depths of the woods and even isolated from the life of the century.

Yes, I have loved as none in the world ever loved—with an insensate and furious passion—so violent that I am astonished it did not cause my heart to burst asunder. Ah, what nights—what nights!

From my earliest childhood I had felt a vocation to the priesthood, so that all my studies were directed with that idea in view. Up to the age of twenty-four my life had been only a prolonged novitiate. Having completed my course of theology I successively received all the minor orders, and my superiors judged me worthy, despite my youth, to pass the last awful degree. My ordination was fixed for Easter week.

I had never gone into the world. My world was confined by the walls of the college and the seminary. I knew in a vague sort of a way that there was something called Woman, but I never permitted my thoughts to dwell on such a subject, and I lived in a state of perfect innocence. Twice a year only I saw my infirm and aged mother, and in those visits were comprised my sole relations with the outer world.

I regretted nothing; I felt not the least hesitation at taking the last irrevocable step; I was filled with joy and impatience. Never did a betrothed lover count the slow hours with more feverish ardor; I slept only to dream that I was saying mass; I believed there could be nothing in the world more delightful than to be a priest; I would have refused to be a king or a poet in preference. My ambition could conceive of no loftier aim.

I tell you this in order to show you that what happened to me could not have happened in the natural order of things, and to enable you to understand that I was the victim of an inexplicable fascination.

At last the great day came. I walked to the church with a step so light that I fancied myself sustained in air, or that I had wings upon my shoulders. I believed myself an angel, and wondered at the sombre and thoughtful faces of my companions, for there were several of us. I had passed all the night in prayer, and was in a condition well nigh bordering on ecstasy. The bishop, a venerable old man, seemed to me God the Father leaning over his Eternity, and I beheld Heaven through the vault of the temple.

You well know the details of that ceremony—the benediction, the communion under both forms, the anointing of the palms of the hands with the Oil of Catechumens, and then the holy sacrifice offered in concert with the bishop.

Ah, truly spake Job when he declared that the imprudent man is one who hath not made a covenant with his eyes! I accidentally lifted my head, which until then I had kept down, and beheld before me, so close that it seemed that I could have touched her—although she was actually a considerable distance from me and on the further side of the sanctuary railing—a young woman of extraordinary beauty and attired with royal magnificence. It seemed as though scales had suddenly fallen from my eyes. I felt like a blind man who unexpectedly recovers his sight. The bishop, so radiantly glorious but an instant before, suddenly vanished away, the tapers paled upon their golden candlesticks like stars in the dawn, and a vast darkness seemed to fill the whole church. The charming creature appeared in bright relief against the background of that darkness, like some angelic revelation. She seemed herself radiant, and radiating light rather than receiving it.

I lowered my eyelids, firmly resolved not to again open them, that I might not be influenced by external objects, for distraction had gradually taken possession of me until I hardly knew what I was doing.

In another minute, nevertheless, I reopened my eyes, for through my eyelashes I still beheld her, all sparkling with prismatic colors, and surrounded with such a purple penumbra as one beholds in gazing at the sun.

Oh, how beautiful she was! The greatest painters, who followed ideal beauty into heaven itself, and thence brought back to earth the true portrait of the Madonna, never in their delineations even approached that wildly beautiful reality which I saw before me. Neither the verses of the poet nor the palette of the artist could convey any conception of her. She was rather tall, with a form and bearing of a goddess. Her hair, of a soft blonde hue, was parted in the midst and flowed back over her temples in two rivers of rippling gold; she seemed a diademed queen. Her forehead, bluish white in its transparency, extended its calm breadth above the arches of her eyebrows, which by a strange singularity were almost black, and admirably relieved the effect of seagreen eyes of unsustainable vivacity and brilliancy. What eyes! With a single flash they could have decided a man's destiny. They had a life, a limpidity, an ardor, a humid light which I have never seen in human eyes; they shot forth rays like arrows, which I could distinctly see enter my heart. I know not if the fire which illumined them came from heaven or from hell, but assuredly it came from one or the other. That woman was either an angel or a demon, perhaps both. Assuredly she never sprang from the flank of Eve, our common mother.

What happens here is beyond "the *natural* order of things." The bishop and the church form a symmetrical binarism with Clarimonde, the house and minister of God on one hand, the pagan goddess on the other. She seems to appear as the other of the Church, but from *within* it, and the she quickly assumes such radiance and immediacy that the whole binarism is submerged in her presence. She must be "The Eternal Haunter" of Hearn's essay, the goddess of the Tree of Life: "Seek to woo her—she is Echo. Seek to clasp her—she is Shadow. But her smile will haunt you into the hour of dissolution and beyond" (*Exotics*, p. 298). However,

occasionally phantom women figure in [Japanese] picture-books in the likeness of living women; but these are not true ghosts. They are fox-women or other goblins; and their supernatural character is suggested by a peculiar expression of the eyes and a certain impossible elfish grace. (*Glimpses*, p. 428)

Her appearance and the priest's infatuation (two phenomena that are not distinct), are possible because he has not "made a covenant" with his eyes. A figure of his own desire and of the Church's repressed voluptuary nature, Clarimonde is a manifestation of the self's—here the body's—nonintegrity—the eyes' discrepant relation to the will. Her continued appearance, and Romuald's desire, depend on this nonintegrity, which dissolves the binarism of un/natural. But neither Clarimonde nor Romuald's desire necessarily threatens the Church, or Romuald's soul. It is not accidental that this scene of infatuation occurs within the precincts of the Church.

Teeth of the most lustrous pearl gleamed in her ruddy smile, and at every inflection of her lips little dimples appeared in the satiny rose of her adorable cheeks. There was a delicacy and pride in the regal outline of her nostrils bespeaking noble blood. Agate gleams played over the smooth lustrous skin of her halfbare shoulders, and strings of great blonde pearls—almost equal to her neck in beauty of color—descended upon her bosom. From time to time she elevated her head with the undulating grace of a startled serpent or peacock, thereby imparting a quivering motion to the high lace ruff which surrounded it like a silver trelliswork.

She wore a robe of orange-red velvet, and from her wide erminelined sleeves there peeped forth patrician hands of infinite delicacy, and so ideally transparent that, like the fingers of Aurora, they permitted the light to shine through them.

All these details I can recollect at this moment as plainly as though they were of yesterday, for notwithstanding I was greatly troubled at the time, nothing escaped me; the faintest touch of shading, the little dark speck at the point of the chin, the imperceptible down at the corners of the lips, the velvety floss upon the brow, the quivering shadows of the eyelashes upon the cheeks, I could notice everything with astonishing lucidity of perception.

And gazing I felt opening within me gates that had until then remained closed; vents long obstructed became all clear, permitting glimpses of unfamiliar perspectives within; life suddenly made itself visible to me under a totally novel aspect. I felt as though I had just been born into a new world and a new order of things. A frightful anguish commenced to torture my heart as with red-hot pincers. Every successive minute seemed to me at once but a second and yet a century. Meanwhile the ceremony was proceeding, and I shortly found myself transported far from that world of which my newly-born desires were furiously besieging the entrance. Nevertheless I answered "Yes" when I wished to say "No," though all within me protested against the violence done to my soul by my tongue. Some occult power seemed to force the words from my throat against my will. Thus it is, perhaps, that so many young girls walk to the altar firmly resolved to refuse in a startling manner the husband imposed upon them, and that yet not one ever fulfils her intention. Thus it is, doubtless, that so many poor novices take the veil, though they have resolved to tear it into shreds at the moment when called upon to utter the vows. One dares not thus cause so great a scandal to all present, nor deceive the expectation of so many people. All those eyes, all those wills seem to weigh down upon you like a cope of lead; and, moreover, measures have been so well taken, everything has been so thoroughly arranged beforehand and after a fashion so evidently irrevocable, that the will yields to the weight of circumstances and utterly breaks down.

As the ceremony proceeded the features of the fair unknown changed their expression. Her look had at first been one of caressing tenderness; it changed to an air of disdain and of mortification, as though at not having been able to make itself understood.

With an effort of will sufficient to have uprooted a mountain, I strove to cry out that I would not be a priest, but I could not speak; my tongue seemed nailed to my palate, and I found it impossible to express my will by the least syllable of negation. Though fully awake, I felt like one under the influence of a nightmare, who vainly strives to shriek out the one word upon which life depends.

She seemed conscious of the martyrdom I was undergoing, and, as though to encourage me, she gave me a look replete with divinest promise. Her eyes were a poem; their every glance was a song.

She said to me:

"If thou wilt be mine, I shall make thee happier than God Himself in His paradise. The angels themselves will be jealous of thee. Tear off that funeral shroud in which thou art about to wrap thyself. I am Beauty, I am Youth, I am Life. Come to me! Together we shall be Love. Can Jehovah offer thee aught in exchange? Our lives will flow on like a dream, in one eternal kiss.

"Fling forth the wine of that chalice, and thou art free. I will conduct thee to the Unknown Isles. Thou shalt sleep in my bosom upon a bed of massy gold under a silver pavilion, for I love thee and would take thee

away from thy God, before whom so many noble hearts pour forth floods of love which never reach even the steps of His throne!"

These words seemed to float to my ears in a rhythm of infinite sweetness, for her look was actually sonorous, and the utterances of her eyes were reechoed in the depths of my heart as though living lips had breathed them into my life. I felt myself willing to renounce God, and yet my tongue mechanically fulfilled all the formalities of the ceremony. The fair one gave me another look, so beseeching, so despairing that keen blades seemed to pierce my heart, and I felt my bosom transfixed by more swords than those of Our Lady of Sorrows.

All was consummated; I had become a priest.

Never was deeper anguish painted on human face than upon hers. The maiden who beholds her affianced lover suddenly fall dead at her side, the mother bending over the empty cradle of her child, Eve seated at the threshold of the gate of Paradise, the miser who finds a stone substituted for his stolen treasure, the poet who accidentally permits the only manuscript of his finest work to fall into the fire, could not wear a look so despairing, so inconsolable. All the blood had abandoned her charming face, leaving it whiter than marble; her beautiful arms hung lifelessly on either side of her body as though their muscles had suddenly relaxed, and she sought the support of a pillar, for her yielding limbs almost betrayed her. As for myself, I staggered toward the door of the church, livid as death, my forehead bathed with a sweat bloodier than that of Calvary; I felt as though I were being strangled; the vault seemed to have flattened down upon my shoulders, and it seemed to me that my head alone sustained the whole weight of the dome.

As I was about to cross the threshold a hand suddenly caught mine—a woman's hand! I had never till then touched the hand of any woman. It was cold as a serpent's skin, and yet its impress remained upon my wrist, burnt there as though branded by a glowing iron. It was she. "Unhappy man! Unhappy man! What hast thou done?" she exclaimed in a low voice, and immediately disappeared in the crowd.

The aged bishop passed by. He cast a severe and scrutinizing look upon me. My face presented the wildest aspect imaginable; I blushed and turned pale alternately; dazzling lights flashed before my eyes. A companion took pity on me. He seized my arm and led me out. I could not possibly have found my way back to the seminary unassisted. At the corner of a street, while the young priest's attention was momentarily turned in another direction, a negro page, fantastically garbed, approached me, and without pausing on his way slipped into my hand a little pocketbook with gold-embroidered corners, at the same time giving me a sign to hide it. I concealed it in my sleeve, and there kept it until I found myself alone in my cell. Then I opened the clasp. There were only two leaves within, bearing the words, "Clarimonde. At the Concini Palace." So little acquainted was I at that time with the things of this world that I had never heard of Clarimonde, celebrated as she was, and I had no idea as to where the Concini Palace was situated. I hazarded a thousand conjectures, each more extravagant than the last; but, in truth, I cared little whether she were a great lady or a courtesan, so that I could but see her once more.

My love, although the growth of a single hour, had taken imperishable root. I did not even dream of attempting to tear it up, so fully was I convinced such a thing would be impossible. That woman had completely taken possession of me. One look from her had sufficed to change my very nature. She had breathed her will into my life, and I no longer lived in myself, but in her and for her. I gave myself up to a thousand extravagancies. I kissed the place upon my hand which she had touched, and I repeated her name over and over again for hours in succession. I only needed to close my eyes in order to see her distinctly as though she were actually present; and I reiterated to myself the words she had uttered in my ear at the church porch: "Unhappy man! Unhappy man! What hast thou done?" I comprehended at last the full horror of my situation, and the funereal and awful restraints of the state into which I had just entered became clearly revealed to me. To be a priest!—that is, to be chaste, to never love, to observe no distinction of sex or age, to turn from the sight of all beauty, to put out one's own eyes, to hide forever crouching in the chill shadows of some church or cloister, to visit none but the dying, to watch by unknown corpses, and ever bear about with one the black soutane as a garb of mourning for one's self, so that your very dress might serve as a pall for your coffin.

And I felt life rising within me like a subterranean lake, expanding and overflowing; my blood leaped fiercely through my arteries; my long-restrained youth suddenly burst into active being, like the aloe which blooms but once in a hundred years, and then bursts into blossom with a clap of thunder.

What could I do in order to see Clarimonde once more? I had no pretext to offer for desiring to leave the seminary, not knowing any person in the city. I would not even be able to remain there but a short time, and was only waiting my assignment to the curacy which I must thereafter occupy. I tried to remove the bars of the window; but it was at a fearful height from the ground, and I found that as I had no ladder it would be useless to think of escaping thus. And, furthermore, I could descend thence only by night in any event, and afterward how should I be able to find my way through the inextricable labyrinth of streets? All these difficulties, which to many would have appeared altogether insignificant, were gigantic to me, a poor seminarist who had fallen in love only the day before for the first time, without experience, without money, without attire.

"Ah!" cried I to myself in my blindness, "were I not a priest I could have seen her every day; I might have been her lover, her spouse. Instead of being wrapped in this dismal shroud of mine I would have had garments of silk and velvet, golden chains, a sword, and fair plumes like other handsome young cavaliers. My hair, instead of being dishonored by the tonsure, would flow down upon my neck in waving curls; I would have a fine waxed mustache; I would be a gallant." But one hour passed before an altar, a few hastily articulated words, had forever cut me off from the number of the living, and I had myself sealed down the stone of my own tomb; I had with my own hand bolted the gate of my prison!

I went to the window. The sky was beautifully blue; the trees had donned their spring robes; nature seemed to be making parade of an ironical joy. The Place was filled with people, some going, others coming; young beaux and young beauties were sauntering in couples toward the groves and gardens; merry youths passed by, cheerily trolling refrains of drinking songs—it was all a picture of vivacity, life, animation, gayety, which formed a bitter contrast with my mourning and my solitude. On the steps of the gate sat a young mother playing with her child. She kissed its little rosy mouth still impearled with drops of milk, and performed, in order to amuse it, a thousand divine little puerilities such as only mothers know how to invent. The father standing at a little distance smiled gently upon the charming group, and with folded arms seemed to hug his joy to his heart. I could not endure that spectacle. I closed the window with violence, and flung myself on my bed, my heart filled with frightful hate and jealousy, and gnawed my fingers and my bedcovers like a tiger that has passed ten days without food.

I know not how long I remained in this condition, but at last, while writing on the bed in a fit of spasmodic fury, I suddenly perceived the Abbé Sérapion, who was standing erect in the centre of the room, watching me attentively. Filled with shame of myself, I let my head fall upon my breast and covered my face with my hands.

"Romuald, my friend, something very extraordinary is transpiring within you," observed Sérapion, after a few moments' silence; "your conduct is altogether inexplicable. You—always so quiet, so pious, so gentle—you to rage in your cell like a wild beast! Take heed, brother—do not listen to the suggestions of the devil. The Evil Spirit, furious that you have consecrated yourself forever to the Lord, is prowling around you like a ravening wolf and making a last effort to obtain possession of you. Instead of allowing yourself to be conquered, my dear Romuald, make to yourself a cuirass of prayers, a buckler of mortifications, and combat the enemy like a valiant man; you will then assuredly overcome him. Virtue must be proved by temptation, and gold comes forth purer from the hands of the assayer. Fear not. Never allow yourself to become discouraged. The most watchful and steadfast souls are at moments liable to such temptation. Pray, fast, meditate, and the Evil Spirit will depart from you."

The vision of Clarimonde coincides with Romuald's vows, while it seems to compromise them, to embody his doubts. But he realizes the sight of her as a *koan*: it is accompanied by a "perfect lucidity of perception," a kind of *satori* or instant of blinding insight into Romuald's own nature, and that of the Church.

Sérapion defends the binarism that places nature and artifice, evil and good, on opposite sides; he opposes the "perfect lucidity" of doubt and nonintegrity of self. He might be compared to a Jesuit missionary landing on the shores of Japan, confronted by the pagan (Shinto) Sun-Goddess, Amaterasu, and pronouncing her a "demon." To his mind, Clarimonde (like Amaterasu) embodies the limitations of Western dualism, according to which everything must be always divided, whether between good and evil, or artifice and nature, subject and object, matter and spirit, life and death. Yet the vampire is both dead and alive, and neither. In this she is like a book, representing the great paradox of human being: mere matter, ink and paper, on the one hand, pure ether, mind, imagination, on the other. Somehow Clarimonde—like Hearn's Japan—resolves these two irresolvable opposites into one irresistible object of desire, which perfectly requites the desire focused on it.

Clarimonde arises directly out of the distance that Sérapion, sober cleric, places between himself-as-subject and the object-world, between life and death, between human artifice and nature, and she mocks the Christian promise ("the spirit made flesh") of bodily resurrection because she does not need it—her undeadness makes the Christian "redemption" of matter *moot*, unnecessary, superfluous. Both alive and dead, she is the perfect figure for the distance separating each term of every dualism, and yet she threatens, by the violence of desire she inspires and embodies (love is the most violently intense of all "artificial realities," and perhaps the most powerful *koan*), to blur the differences sustaining all dualisms.

Any vampire is a figure for human being as permanently material, physically immutable, and also for the worst sort of "objectification," the use or consumption of human beings as mere objects (for their physical "essence," their blood). In perfectly reciprocal love, however, such as we are told exists between Clarimonde and Romuald, the difference separating spirit from body, holy love from fleshly lust, is made to vacillate, hover on the brink of disappearance, and the figure of the latter, the vampire, threatens to engulf the very dualism that imagined her, projected her as an embodiment of "evil" (loss of self) in the first place. So to Sérapion, as to any missionary confronting some "oriental" pagan, if Clarimonde cannot be made to seem repugnant, she must be destroyed. Otherwise, if allowed to flourish, she must eventually make Sérapion—who throughout the story is a clerical Sherlock Holmes, embodiment of the *res cogito*, the subject-who-is-supposed-to-know—disappear. The story can only continue for as long as the tension between Sérapion and Clarimonde, master intellect and unintelligible mystery, and can only end with her disappearance. Such is the narrative imperative: what is unintelligible must be "solved" or destroyed.

The words of the Abbé Sérapion restored me to myself, and I became a little more calm. "I came," he continued, "to tell you that you have been appointed to the curacy of C. The priest who had charge of it has just died, and Monseigneur the Bishop has ordered me to have you installed there at once. Be ready, therefore, to start tomorrow." I responded with an inclination of the head, and the Abbé retired. I opened my missal and commenced reading some prayers, but the letters became confused and blurred under my eyes, the thread of the ideas entangled itself hopelessly in my brain, and the volume at last fell from my hands without my being aware of it.

To leave tomorrow without having been able to see her again, to add yet another barrier to the many already interposed between us, to lose forever all hope of being able to meet her, except, indeed, through a miracle! Even to write her, alas! would be impossible, for by whom could I despatch my letter? With my sacred character of priest, to whom could I dare unbosom myself, in whom could I confide? I became a prey to the bitterest anxiety.

Then suddenly recurred to me the words of the Abbé Sérapion regarding the artifices of the devil; and the strange character of the adventure, the supernatural beauty of Clarimonde, the phosphoric light of her eyes, the burning imprint of her hand, the agony into which she had thrown me, the sudden change wrought within me when all my piety vanished in a single instant—these and other things clearly testified to the work of the Evil One, and perhaps that satiny hand was but the glove which concealed his claws. Filled with terror at these fancies, I again picked up the missal which had slipped from my knees and fallen upon the floor, and once more gave myself up to prayer.

Next morning Sérapion came to take me away. Two mules freighted with our miserable valises awaited us at the gate. He mounted one, and I the other as well as I knew how.

As we passed along the streets of the city, I gazed attentively at all the windows and balconies in the hope of seeing Clarimonde, but it was yet early in the morning, and the city had hardly opened its eyes. Mine sought to penetrate the blinds and window curtains of all the palaces before which we were passing. Sérapion doubtless attributed this curiosity to my admiration of the architecture, for he slackened the pace of his animal in order to give me time to look around me. At last we passed the city gates and commenced to mount the hill beyond. When we arrived at its summit I turned to take a last look at the place where Clarimonde dwelt. The shadow of a great cloud hung over all the city; the contrasting colors of its blue and red roofs were lost in the uniform half-tint, through which here and there floated upward, like white flakes of foam, the smoke of freshly kindled fires. By a singular optical effect one edifice, which surpassed in height all the neighboring buildings that were still dimly veiled by the vapors, towered up, fair and lustrous with the gilding of a solitary beam of sunlight—although actually more than a league away it seemed quite near. The smallest details of its architecture were plainly distinguishable—the turrets, the platforms, the window-casements, and even the swallow-tailed weather vanes.

"*What is that palace I see over there, all lighted up by the sun?*" *I asked Sérapion. He shaded his eyes with his hand, and having looked in the direction indicated, replied: "It is the ancient palace which the Prince Concini has given to the courtesan Clarimonde. Awful things are done there!"*

At that instant, I know not yet whether it was a reality or an illusion, I fancied I saw gliding along the terrace a shapely white figure, which gleamed for a moment in passing and as quickly vanished. It was Clarimonde.

Oh, did she know that at that very hour, all feverish and restless—from the height of the rugged road which separated me from her and which, alas! I could never more descend—I was directing my eyes upon the palace where she dwelt, and which a mocking beam of sunlight seemed to bring nigh to me, as though inviting me to enter therein as its lord? Undoubtedly she must have known it, for her soul was too sympathetically united with mine not to have felt its least emotional thrill, and that subtle sympathy it must have been which prompted her to climb—although clad only in her nightdress—to the summit of the terrace, amid the icy dews of the morning.

The shadow gained the palace, and the scene became to the eye only a motionless ocean of roofs and gables, amid which one mountainous undulation was distinctly visible. Sérapion urged his mule forward, my own at once followed at the same gait, and a sharp angle in the road at last hid the city of S forever from my eyes, as I was destined never to return thither. At the close of a weary threedays' journey through dismal country fields, we caught sight of the cock upon the steeple of the church which I was to take charge of, peeping above the trees, and after having followed some winding roads fringed with thatched cottages and little gardens, we found ourselves in front of the façade, which certainly possessed few features of magnificence. A porch ornamented with some mouldings, and two or three pillars rudely hewn from sandstone; a tiled roof with counterforts of the same sandstone as the pillars, that was all. To the left lay the cemetery, overgrown with high weeds, and having a great iron cross rising up in its centre; to the right stood the presbytery, under the shadow of the church. It was a house of the most extreme simplicity and frigid cleanliness. We entered the enclosure. A few chickens were picking up some oats scattered upon the ground; accustomed, seemingly, to the black habit of ecclesiastics, they showed no fear of our presence and scarcely troubled themselves to get out of our way. A hoarse, wheezy barking fell upon our ears, and we saw an aged dog running toward us.

It was my predecessor's dog. He had dull bleared eyes, grizzled hair, and every mark of the greatest age to which a dog can possibly attain. I patted him gently, and he proceeded at once to march along beside me with an air of satisfaction unspeakable. A very old woman, who had been the housekeeper of the former curé, also came to meet us, and after having invited me into a little back parlor, asked whether I intended to retain her. I replied that I would take care of her, and the dog, and the chickens, and all the furniture her master had bequeathed her at his death. At this she became fairly transported with joy, and the Abbé Sérapion at once paid her the price which she asked for her little property. As soon as my installation was over, the Abbé Sérapion returned to the seminary. I was, therefore, left alone, with no one but myself to look to for aid or counsel. The thought of Clarimonde again began to haunt me, and in spite of all my endeavors to banish it, I always found it present in my meditations. One evening, while promenading in my little garden along the walks bordered with boxplants, I fancied that I saw through the elm-trees the figure of a woman, who followed my every movement, and that I beheld two sea-green eyes gleaming through the foliage; but it was only an illusion, and on going round to the other side of the garden, I could find nothing except a footprint on the sanded walk—a footprint so small that it seemed to have been made by the foot of a child.

Then I notice how small and shapely the feet of the people are,—whether bare brown feet of peasants, or beautiful feet of children wearing tiny, tiny geta, or feet of young girls in snowy tabi. The tabi, the white digitated stocking, gives to a small light foot a mythological aspect,—the white cleft grace of the foot of a fauness. Clad or bare, the Japanese foot has the antique symmetry: it has not yet been distorted by the infamous foot-gear which has deformed the feet of Occidentals ("My First Day in the Orient," *Glimpses*, pp. 10–11).

The garden was enclosed by very high walls. I searched every nook and corner of it, but could discover no one there. I have never succeeded in fully accounting for this circumstance, which, after all, was nothing compared with the strange things which happened to me afterward.

For a whole year I lived thus, filling all the duties of my calling with the most scrupulous exactitude, praying and fasting, exhorting and lending ghostly aid to the sick [Nothing like the word *ghostly* appears in the French text—this is an addition reflecting Hearn's own style and preoccupations. Such small changes occur throughout. While mostly hewing closely to the locutions of Gautier's original, Hearn imbues the text with his own voice.] *and bestowing alms even to the extent of frequently depriving myself of the very necessaries of life. But I felt a great aridness within me, and the sources of grace seemed closed against me. I never found that happiness which should spring from the fulfilment of a holy mission; my thoughts were far away, and the words of Clarimonde were ever upon my lips like an involuntary refrain. Oh, brother, meditate well on this! Through having but once lifted my eyes to look upon a woman, through one fault apparently so venial, I have for years remained a victim to the most miserable agonies, and the happiness of my life has been destroyed forever.* [Unhappiness, in this formulation is the result of recognizing the other within the precinct of the same—it is the other side of *satori, satori* misunderstood, feared or gone awry.]

I will not longer dwell upon those defeats, or on those inward victories invariably followed by yet more terrible falls, but will at once proceed to the facts of my story. One night my doorbell was long and violently rung. The aged housekeeper arose and opened to the stranger, and the figure of a man, whose complexion was deeply bronzed, and who was richly clad in a foreign costume, with a poniard at his girdle, appeared under the rays of Barbara's lantern. Her first impulse was one of terror, but the stranger reassured her, and stated that he desired to see me at once on matters relating to my holy calling. Barbara invited him upstairs, where I was on the point of retiring. The stranger told me that his mistress, a very noble lady, was lying at the point of death, and desired to see a priest. I replied that I was prepared to follow him, took with me the sacred articles necessary for extreme unction, and descended in all haste. Two horses black as the night itself stood without the gate, pawing the ground with impatience, and veiling their chests with long streams of smoky vapor [It is interesting that this very Hearnian image is not Hearn's, but translated directly from Gautier—perhaps a testimony to the extent to which Hearn's own distinctive style was shaped by his translations.] *exhaled from their nostrils. He held the stirrup and aided me to mount upon one; then, merely laying his hand upon the pummel of the saddle, he vaulted on the other, pressed the animal's sides with his knees, and loosened rein. The horse bounded forward with the velocity of an arrow. Mine, of which the stranger held the bridle, also started off at a*

*swift gallop, keeping up with his companion. We devoured the road. The
ground flowed backward beneath us in a long streaked line of pale gray,
and the black silhouettes of the trees seemed fleeing by us on either side
like an army in rout. We passed through a forest so profoundly gloomy
that I felt my flesh creep in the chill darkness with superstitious fear. The
showers of bright sparks which flew from the stony road under the iron-
shod feet of our horses, remained glowing in our wake like a fiery trail;
and had anyone at that hour of the night beheld us both—my guide and
myself—he must have taken us for two spectres riding upon nightmares.*

This passage demands juxtaposition with another one from Hearn's
"First Day in the Orient:"

I lie down to sleep, and I dream. I see Chinese texts—multitudi-
nous, weird, mysterious—fleeing by me, all in one direction; ideographs white and dark, upon sign-boards, upon paper screens,
upon backs of sandaled men. They seem to live, these ideographs,
with conscious life; they are moving their parts, moving with a
movement as of insects, monstrously, like *phasmidae*. I am rolling
always through low, narrow, luminous streets in a phantom jinri-
kisha, whose wheels make no sound. (*Glimpses*, p. 28)

*Witch fires ever and anon flitted across the road before us, and the night-
birds shrieked fearsomely in the depth of the woods beyond, where we beheld at intervals glow the phosphorescent eyes of wildcats. The manes of
the horses became more and more dishevelled, the sweat streamed over
their flanks, and their breath came through their nostrils hard and fast.
But when he found them slacking pace, the guide reanimated them by uttering a strange, guttural, unearthly cry, and the gallop recommenced
with fury. At last the whirlwind race ceased; a huge black mass pierced
through with many bright points of light suddenly rose before us, the
hoofs of our horses echoed louder upon a strong wooden drawbridge, and
we rode under a great vaulted archway which darkly yawned between
two enormous towers. Some great excitement evidently reigned in the
castle. Servants with torches were crossing the courtyard in every direction, and above lights were ascending and descending from landing to
landing. I obtained a confused glimpse of vast masses of architecture—
columns, arcades, flights of steps, stairways—a royal voluptuousness
and elfin magnificence of construction worthy of fairyland. A negro*

page—the same who had before brought me the tablet from Clarimonde, and whom I instantly recognized—approached to aid me in dismounting, and the majordomo, attired in black velvet with a gold chain about his neck, advanced to meet me, supporting himself upon an ivory cane. Large tears were falling from his eyes and streaming over his cheeks and white beard. "Too late!" he cried, sorrowfully shaking his venerable head. "Too late, sir priest! But if you have not been able to save the soul, come at least to watch by the poor body."

He took my arm and conducted me to the death chamber. I wept not less bitterly than he, for I had learned that the dead one was none other than that Clarimonde whom I had so deeply and so wildly loved. A prie-dieu stood at the foot of the bed; a bluish flame flickering in a bronze patera filled all the room with a wan, deceptive light, here and there bringing out in the darkness at intervals some projection of furniture or cornice. In a chiselled urn upon the table there was a faded white rose, whose leaves—excepting one that still held—had all fallen, like odorous tears, to the foot of the vase. A broken black mask, a fan, and disguises of every variety, which were lying on the armchairs, bore witness that death had entered suddenly and unannounced into that sumptuous dwelling. Without daring to cast my eyes upon the bed, I knelt down and commenced to repeat the Psalms for the Dead, with exceeding fervor, thanking God that he had placed the tomb between me and the memory of this woman, so that I might thereafter be able to utter her name in my prayers as a name forever sanctified by death. But! my fervor gradually weakened, and I fell insensibly into a reverie. That chamber bore no semblance to a chamber of death. In lieu of the fetid and cadaverous odors which I had been accustomed to breathe during such funereal vigils, a languorous vapor of Oriental perfume—I know not what amorous odor of woman—softly floated through the tepid air. That pale light seemed rather a twilight gloom contrived for voluptuous pleasure, than a substitute for the yellow-flickering watch-tapers which shine by the side of corpses. I thought upon the strange destiny which enabled me to meet Clarimonde again at the very moment when she was lost to me forever, and a sigh of regretful anguish escaped from my breast. Then it seemed to me that some one behind me had also sighed, and I turned round to look. It was only an echo. But in that moment my eyes fell upon the bed of death which they had till then avoided. The red damask curtains decorated with large flowers worked in embroidery, and looped up with gold bullion, permitted me to behold the fair dead lying at full length, with hands joined on her bosom. She was covered with a linen wrapping of dazzling whiteness, which seemed a strong contrast with the gloomy purple of the hangings, and was of so fine a texture that it concealed nothing of her body's charming form, and allowed the eye to follow those beautiful outlines—undulating like the neck of a swan—which even death had not robbed of their supple grace. She seemed an alabaster statue executed by some skilful sculptor to place upon the tomb of a queen, or rather, perhaps, like a slumbering maiden over whom the silent snow had woven a spotless veil.

Here as nowhere else in the text it is clear that Clarimonde represents art *and* nature, their nondistinction, just as in the streets of Japan Hearn found the living art of Hiroshige and Hokusai. This is not necroeroticism; it is not about ordinary death (it does not smell, or look like death) but rather art and life realized in one "object" who is also a subject—a living, breathing, but "dead" *res cogito*. This is "undeath." One can only wonder about the resonances for Hearn in this passage: the dead beauty of classical Greece he found entombed in his aunt's library, the same surreal beauty he would later find in the artificial worlds of writers such as Gautier and Loti, and then in Japanese streets and Japanese faces, even Japanese ghosts.

I could no longer maintain my constrained attitude of prayer. The air of the alcove intoxicated me, that febrile perfume of half-faded roses penetrated my very brain, and I commenced to pace restlessly up and down the chamber, pausing at each turn before the bier to contemplate the graceful corpse lying beneath the transparency of its shroud. Wild fancies came thronging to my brain. I thought to myself that she might not, perhaps, be really dead; that she might only have feigned death for the purpose of bringing me to her castle, and then declaring her love. At one time I even thought I saw her foot move under the whiteness of the coverings, and slightly disarrange the long, straight folds of the winding sheet.

And then I asked myself: "Is this indeed Clarimonde? What proof have I that it is she? [Clarimonde is discontinuous *even with herself.*] *Might not that black page have passed into the service of some other lady? Surely, I must be going mad to torture and afflict myself thus!" But my heart answered with a fierce throbbing: "It is she; it is she indeed!" I approached the bed again, and fixed my eyes with redoubled attention upon the object of my incertitude. Ah, must I confess it? That exquisite perfection of bodily form, although purified and made sacred by the shadow of death, affected me more voluptuously than it should have done, and that repose so closely resembled slumber that one might well have mistaken it for such. I forgot that I had come there to perform a funeral ceremony; I fancied myself a young bridegroom entering the chamber of the bride, who all modestly hides her fair face, and through coyness seeks to keep herself wholly veiled. Heartbroken with grief, yet wild with hope, shuddering at once with fear and pleasure, I bent over her and grasped the corner of the sheet. I lifted it back, holding my breath all the while through fear of waking her. My arteries throbbed with such violence that I felt them hiss through my temples, and the sweat poured from my forehead in streams, as though I had lifted a mighty slab of marble. There, indeed, lay Clarimonde, even as I had seen her at the church on the day of my ordination. She was not less charming than then. With her, death seemed but a last coquetry. The pallor of her cheeks, the less brilliant carnation of her lips, her long eyelashes lowered and relieving their dark fringe against that white skin, lent her an unspeakably seductive aspect of melancholy chastity and mental suffering; her long loose hair, still intertwined with some little blue flowers, made a shining pillow for her head, and veiled the nudity of her shoulders with its thick ringlets; her beautiful hands, purer, more diaphanous than the Host, were crossed on her bosom in an attitude of pious rest and silent prayer, which served to counteract all that might have proven otherwise too alluring—even after death—in the exquisite roundness and ivory polish of her bare arms from which the pearl bracelets had not yet been removed. I remained long in mute contemplation, and the more I gazed, the less could I persuade myself that life had really abandoned that beautiful body forever. I do not know whether it was an illusion or a reflection of the lamplight, but it seemed to me that the blood was again commencing to circulate under that lifeless pallor, although she remained all motionless. I laid my hand lightly on her arm; it was cold, but not colder than her hand on the day when it touched mine at the portals of the church. I resumed my position, bending my face above her, and bathing her cheeks with the warm dew of my tears. Ah, what bitter feelings of despair and helplessness, what agonies unutterable did I endure in that long watch! Vainly did I wish that I could have gathered all my life into one mass that I might give it all to her, and breathe into her chill remains the flame which devoured me. The night advanced, and feeling the moment of eternal separation approach, I could not deny myself the last sad sweet pleasure of imprinting a kiss upon the dead lips of her who had been my only*

love . . . Oh, miracle! A faint breath mingled itself with my breath, and
the mouth of Clarimonde responded to the passionate pressure of mine.
Her eyes unclosed, and lighted up with something of their former bril-
liancy; she uttered a long sigh, and uncrossing her arms passed them
around my neck with a look of ineffable delight." Ah, it is thou, Romu-
ald!" she murmured in a voice languishingly sweet as the last vibrations
of a harp. "What ailed thee, dearest? I waited so long for thee that I am
dead; but we are now betrothed; I can see thee and visit thee. Adieu,
Romuald, adieu! I love thee. That is all I wished to tell thee, and I give
thee back the life which thy kiss for a moment recalled. We shall soon
meet again."

Her head fell back, but her arms yet encircled me, as though to re-
tain me still. A furious whirlwind suddenly burst in the window, and
entered the chamber. The last remaining leaf of the white rose for a mo-
ment palpitated at the extremity of the stalk like a butterfly's wing, then
it detached itself and flew forth through the open casement, bearing with
it the soul of Clarimonde. The lamp was extinguished, and I fell insen-
sible upon the bosom of the beautiful dead.

When I came to myself again I was lying on the bed in my little
room at the presbytery, [Again, Clarimonde appears *inside* what is
supposed to be her *outside,* her alterity and distance are exposed
as identity and proximity; and the alternative worlds of the presbytery and the palace inhabit each other's difference.] *and the old*
dog of the former curé was licking my hand which had been hanging
down outside of the covers. Barbara, all trembling with age and anxiety,
was busying herself about the room, opening and shutting drawers, and
emptying powders into glasses. On seeing me open my eyes, the old
woman uttered a cry of joy, the dog yelped and wagged his tail, but I was
still so weak that I could not speak a single word or make the slightest
motion. Afterward I learned that I had lain thus for three days, giving no
evidence of life beyond the faintest respiration. Those three days do not
reckon in my life, nor could I ever imagine whither my spirit had de-
parted during those three days; I have no recollection of aught relating to
them. Barbara told me that the same coppery-complexioned man who
came to seek me on the night of my departure from the presbytery, had
brought me back the next morning in a close[d] litter, and departed im-
mediately afterward. When I became able to collect my scattered
thoughts, I reviewed within my mind all the circumstances of that fateful
night. At first I thought I had been the victim of some magical illusion,

but ere long the recollection of other circumstances, real and palpable in themselves, came to forbid that supposition. I could not believe that I had been dreaming, since Barbara as well as myself had seen the strange man with his two black horses, and described with exactness every detail of his figure and apparel. Nevertheless it appeared that none knew of any castle in the neighborhood answering to the description of that in which I had again found Clarimonde.

One morning I found the Abbé Sérapion in my room.

Sérapion, who pointed out the Concini palace to Romuald, and who knows everything. Perhaps he reminded Lafcadio of his aunt's clerical retainers who censored the picture books he found in her library: in Hearn's view of things the Church usually could be counted on to defame beauty in the name of conscience, to quell nature in the name of human artifice and arrogance, not of art: "The gods had been belied [by the Church] *because* they were beautiful" (*Life and Letters*, p. 24). "This again reminds me of something," wrote Hearn. "When I was a boy I had to go to confession, and my confessions were honest ones. One day I told the ghostly father that I had been guilty of desiring that the devil would come to me in the shape of the beautiful woman in which he came to the anchorites in the desert, and that I thought I should yield to such temptations" (*Life and Letters*, pp. 28–29). Did this really happen, or might the memory have been shaped by Gautier's story? Perhaps it does not matter which came first.

Barbara had advised him that I was ill, and he had come with all speed to see me. Although this haste on his part testified to an affectionate interest in me, yet his visit did not cause me the pleasure which it should have done. The Abbé Sérapion had something penetrating and inquisitorial in his gaze which made me feel very ill at ease. His presence filled me with embarrassment and a sense of guilt. At the first glance he divined my interior trouble, and I hated him for his clairvoyance.

While he inquired after my health in hypocritically honeyed accents, he constantly kept his two great yellow lion-eyes fixed upon me, and plunged his look into my soul like a sounding lead. Then he asked me how I directed my parish, if I was happy in it, how I passed the leisure hours allowed me in the intervals of pastoral duty, whether I had become acquainted with many of the inhabitants of the place, what was my favorite reading, and a thousand other such questions. I answered these inquiries as briefly as possible, and he, without ever waiting for my answers, passed rapidly from one subject of query to another. That conversation had evidently no connection with what he actually wished to say. At last, without any premonition, but as though repeating a piece of news which he had recalled on the instant, and feared might otherwise be forgotten subsequently, he suddenly said, in a clear vibrant voice, which rang in my ears like the trumpets of the Last Judgment: "The great courtesan Clarimonde died a few days ago, at the close of an orgie which lasted eight days and eight nights. It was something infernally splendid. The abominations of the banquets of Belshazzar and Cleopatra were reen-acted there. Good God, what age are we living in? The guests were served by swarthy slaves who spoke an unknown tongue [my emphasis], *and who seemed to me to be veritable demons. The livery of the very least among them would have served for the gala-dress of an emperor. There have always been very strange stories told of this Clarimonde, and all her lovers came to a violent or miserable end. They used to say that she was a ghoul, a female vampire; but I believe she was none other than Beelzebub himself."*

He ceased to speak and commenced to regard me more attentively than ever, as though to observe the effect of his words on me. I could not refrain from starting when I heard him utter the name of Clarimonde, and this news of her death, in addition to the pain it caused me by reason of its coincidence with the nocturnal scenes I had witnessed, filled me with an agony and terror which my face betrayed, despite my utmost en-deavors to appear composed. Sérapion fixed an anxious and severe look upon me, and then observed: "My son, I must warn you that you are standing with foot raised upon the brink of an abyss; take heed lest you fall therein. Satan's claws are long, and tombs are not always true to their trust. The tombstone of Clarimonde should be sealed down with a triple seal, for, if report be true, it is not the first time she has died."

"Not the first time she has died"—an idea echoed in Proust, not of vampires but ordinary mortals, and a commonplace in Buddhist thought: Death as process, not event, essential and present in all the events of a life, beginnings and endings. Or in terms of biology (Hearn was fond of "scientific" analogies), the body dies to itself many times in a lifetime, replacing every living cell over and over, so that even in this life, the purely physical body is not the same over time. Here, in the words of Sérapion, Clarimonde is shown to represent Death as the *failure of closure*, rather than the seal of eternal quiescence (which it "ought" properly to represent), life that endures even in death, and death which will not die.

"May God watch over you, Romuald!"

And with these words the Abbé walked slowly to the door. I did not see him again at that time, for he left for S almost immediately.

I became completely restored to health and resumed my accustomed duties. The memory of Clarimonde and the words of the old Abbé were constantly in my mind; nevertheless no extraordinary event had occurred to verify the funereal predictions of Sérapion, and I had commenced to believe that his fears and my own terrors were overexaggerated, when one night I had a strange dream. I had hardly fallen asleep when I heard my bed-curtains drawn apart, as their rings slided back upon the curtain rod with a sharp sound. I rose up quickly upon my elbow, and beheld the shadow of a woman standing erect before me. I recognized Clarimonde immediately. She bore in her hand a little lamp, shaped like those which are placed in tombs, and its light lent her fingers a rosy transparency, which extended itself by lessening degrees even to the opaque and milky whiteness of her bare arm. Her only garment was the linen winding-sheet which had shrouded her when lying upon the bed of death. She sought to gather its folds over her bosom as though ashamed of being so scantily clad, but her little hand was not equal to the task. She was so white that the color of the drapery blended with that of her flesh under the pallid rays of the lamp. Enveloped with this subtle tissue which betrayed all the contour of her body, she seemed rather the marble statue of some fair antique bather than a woman endowed with life. But dead or living, statue or woman, shadow or body, her beauty was still the same [my emphasis], *only that the green light of her eyes was less brilliant, and her mouth, once so warmly crimson, was only tinted with a faint tender rosiness, like that of her cheeks. The little blue flowers which I had noticed entwined in her hair were withered and dry, and had lost nearly all their leaves, but this did not prevent her from being charming—so charming that notwithstanding the strange character of the adventure, and the unexplainable manner in which she had entered my room, I felt not even for a moment the least fear.*

She placed the lamp on the table and seated herself at the foot of my bed; then bending toward me, she said, in that voice at once silvery clear and yet velvety in its sweet softness, such as I never heard from any lips save hers:

> *"I have kept thee long in waiting, dear Romuald, and it must have seemed to thee that I had forgotten thee. But I come from afar off, very far off, and from a land whence no other has ever yet returned. There is neither sun nor moon in that land whence I come: all is but space and shadow; there is neither road nor pathway: no earth for the foot, no air for the wing; and nevertheless behold me here, for Love is stronger than Death and must conquer him in the end."*

Clarimonde is here the story itself, art itself, but not Pygmalion, because she is as far as anyone knows her own author, and not the by-product of another's narcissism. "Dead or living, statue or woman, shadow or body," she embodies the nondistinction of art and artist, text and writer/reader, phenomena and imagination.

For Hearn, the land in question must—arbitrarily and inevitably—be Japan—not the physical, real Japan, as it is to the Japanese, but as it is for Westerners who have never been there—and remains, for some, like Hearn, even after they see and feel it. The poet James Merrill spoke for such people when he attributed "A chronic ethereality" to Japan. "Given any choice in the matter, [the Japanese] would not exist physically. Neither would their rooms, their clothes, their verses. It is the *idea* of the room (or kimono or haiku), more than any embodiment of it, that has become their triumph" ("The Beaten Path," *Recitative*, p. 145).

> *Oh what sad faces and fearful things I have seen on my way hither! What difficulty my soul, returned to earth through the power of will alone, has had in finding its body and reinstating itself therein! What terrible efforts I had to make ere I could lift the ponderous slab with which they had covered me! See, the palms of my poor hands are all bruised! Kiss them, sweet love, that they may be healed!" She laid the cold palms of her hands upon my mouth, one after the other. I kissed them, indeed, many times, and she the while watched me with a smile of ineffable affection.*
>
> *I confess to my shame that I had entirely forgotten the advice of the Abbé Sérapion and the sacred office wherewith I had been invested. I had fallen without resistance, and at the first assault. I had not even made the least effort to repel the tempter. The fresh coolness of Clarimonde's skin penetrated my own, and I felt voluptuous tremors pass over my whole body. Poor child! in spite of all I saw afterward, I can hardly yet believe*

she was a demon; at least she had no appearance of being such, and never did Satan so skilfully conceal his claws and horns. She had drawn her feet up beneath her, and squatted down on the edge of the couch in an attitude full of negligent coquetry. From time to time she passed her little hand through my hair and twisted it into curls, as though trying how a new style of wearing it would become my face. I abandoned myself to her hands with the most guilty pleasure, while she accompanied her gentle play with the prettiest prattle. The most remarkable fact was that I felt no astonishment whatever at so extraordinary an adventure, and as in dreams one finds no difficulty in accepting the most fantastic events as simple facts, so all these circumstances seemed to me perfectly natural in themselves.

"I lie down to sleep, and I dream. . . . They seem to live, these ideographs, with conscious life; they are moving their parts, moving with conscious life; they are moving their parts, moving with a movement as of insects, monstrously, like *phasmidae*" (Hearn, *Glimpses*, p. 28). Perhaps all objects of desire—which are surely always ideographs, whether people or places—must look this way, if the desire that sees them is strong enough.

"I loved thee long ere I saw thee, dear Romuald, and sought thee everywhere. Thou wast my dream, and I first saw thee in the church at the fatal moment. I said at once, 'It is he!' I gave thee a look into which I threw all the love I ever had, all the love I now have, all the love I shall ever have for thee—a look that would have damned a cardinal or brought a king to his knees at my feet in view of all his court. Thou remainedst unmoved, preferring thy God to me!

"Ah, how jealous I am of that God whom thou didst love and still lovest more than me!

"Woe is me, unhappy one that I am! I can never have thy heart all to myself, I whom thou didst recall to life with a kiss—dead Clarimonde, who for thy sake bursts asunder the gates of the tomb, and comes to consecrate to thee a life which she has resumed only to make thee happy!"

All her words were accompanied with the most impassioned caresses, which bewildered my sense and my reason to such an extent, that I did not fear to utter a frightful blasphemy for the sake of consoling her, and to declare that I loved her as much as God.

Her eyes rekindled and shone like chrysoprases. "In truth?—in very truth?—as much as God!" she cried, flinging her beautiful arms around me. "Since it is so, thou wilt come with me; thou wilt follow me whithersoever I desire. Thou wilt cast away thy ugly black habit. Thou shalt be the proudest and most envied of cavaliers; thou shalt be my lover! To be the acknowledged lover of Clarimonde, who has refused even a Pope, that will be something to feel proud of! Ah, the fair, unspeakably happy existence, the beautiful golden life we shall live together! And when shall we depart, my fair sir?"

"To-morrow! To-morrow!" I cried in my delirium.

"To-morrow, then, so let it be!" she answered. "In the meanwhile I shall have opportunity to change my toilet, for this is a little too light and in nowise suited for a voyage. I must also forthwith notify all my friends who believe me dead, and mourn for me as deeply as they are capable of doing. The money, the dresses, the carriages—all will be ready. I shall call for thee at this same hour. Adieu, dear heart!" And she lightly touched my forehead with her lips. The lamp went out, the curtains closed again, and all became dark; a leaden, dreamless sleep fell on me and held me unconscious until the morning following.

I awoke later than usual, and the recollection of this singular adventure troubled me during the whole day. I finally persuaded myself that it was a mere vapor of my heated imagination. Nevertheless its sensations had been so vivid that it was difficult to persuade myself that they were not real, and it was not without some presentiment of what was going to happen that I got into bed at last, after having prayed God to drive far from me all thoughts of evil, and to protect the chastity of my slumber.

I soon fell into a deep sleep, and my dream was continued. The curtains again parted, and I beheld Clarimonde, not as on the former occasion, pale in her pale windingsheet, with the violets of death upon her cheeks, but gay, sprightly, jaunty, in a superb travelling dress of green velvet, trimmed with gold lace, and looped up on either side to allow a glimpse of satin petticoat. Her blond hair escaped in thick ringlets from beneath a broad black felt hat, decorated with white feathers whimsically twisted into various shapes. In one hand she held a little riding whip terminated by a golden whistle. She tapped me lightly with it, and exclaimed: "Well, my fine sleeper, is this the way you make your preparations? I thought I would find you up and dressed. Arise quickly, we have no time to lose."

I leaped out of bed at once.

"Come, dress yourself, and let us go," she continued, pointing to a little package she had brought with her." The horses are becoming impatient of delay and champing their bits at the door. We ought to have been by this time at least ten leagues distant from here."

I dressed myself hurriedly, and she handed me the articles of apparel herself one by one, bursting into laughter from time to time at my awkwardness, as she explained to me the use of a garment when I had made a mistake. She hurriedly arranged my hair, and this done, held up before me a little pocket mirror of Venetian crystal, rimmed with silver filigree-work, and playfully asked:

"How dost find thyself now? Wilt engage me for thy valet de chambre?"

I was no longer the same person, and I could not even recognize myself. I resembled my former self no more than a finished statue resembles a block of stone. [my emphasis]

So the lover's difference from the object of desire is blurred, and the artist's from the art, the writer from the written, the translator from the translated; artifice and nature are not distinct, or life and death, or art and life.

I resembled my former self no more than a finished statue resembles a block of stone. My old face seemed but a coarse daub of the one reflected in the mirror. I was handsome, and my vanity was sensibly tickled by the metamorphosis. That elegant apparel, that richly embroidered vest had made of me a totally different personage, and I marvelled at the power of transformation owned by a few yards of cloth cut after a certain pattern.

Beauty is a function of artifice, not essence; the self not a self-contained, static entity, but subject to dramatic *intrinsic* metamorphosis simply by being framed and presented differently, by reassembling its pieces in a different order. This is an idea shared by Buddhism and decadence.

The spirit of my costume penetrated my very skin, and within ten minutes more I had become something of a coxcomb.

In order to feel more at ease in my new attire, I took several turns up and down the room. Clarimonde watched me with an air of maternal pleasure, and appeared well satisfied with her work. "Come, enough of this child's play! Let us start, Romuald, dear. We have far to go, and we may not get there in time." She took my hand and led me forth. All the doors opened before her at a touch, and we passed by the dog without awaking him.

At the gate we found Margheritone waiting, the same swarthy groom who had once before been my escort. He held the bridles of three horses, all black like those which bore us to the castle—one for me, one for him, one for Clarimonde. Those horses must have been Spanish genets born of mares fecundated by a zephyr, for they were fleet as the wind itself, and the moon, which had just risen at our departure to light us on the way, rolled over the sky like a wheel detached from her own chariot. We beheld her on the right leaping from tree to tree, and putting herself out of breath in the effort to keep up with us. Soon we came upon a level plain where, hard by a clump of trees, a carriage with four vigorous horses awaited us. We entered it, and the postilions urged their animals into a mad gallop. I had one arm around Clarimonde's waist, and one of her hands clasped in mine; her head leaned upon my shoulder, and I felt her bosom, half bare, lightly pressing against my arm. I had never known such intense happiness. In that hour I had forgotten everything, and I no more remembered having ever been a priest than I remembered what I had been doing in my mother's womb, so great was the fascination which the evil spirit exerted upon me. From that night my nature seemed in some sort to have become halved, and there were two men within me, neither of whom knew the other. At one moment I believed myself a priest who dreamed nightly that he was a gentleman, at another that I was a gentleman who dreamed he was a priest.

There is a practice called "dream yoga" in tantric Buddhism, in which the practitioner learns to recognize dreams while in them, and to manipulate their progress—rather as though composing fiction in the first person. Eventually this leads to an awareness that waking experience can be similarly manipulated, though it requires a greater degree of subtlety and patience to do so, on account of comprising more resistant material constraints than dreams (or paper). I have been suggesting throughout this book that literature, reading and writing, can serve this practice as well or better than dreams. The practice leads to realization that waking experience and dream—or literary experience—are not so different as we are accustomed to think. One illusion requires only waking, or closing the book, to arrest it, and the other death, but this may not be an absolute difference. Sérapion and the Church here stand for the elements of Western thought that insist on keeping this distinction more or less absolute. Romuald's carefully constructed, complex, intellectually and scholastically grounded illusion of static, univocal "selfhood" is coming undone at the hands of Clarimonde, whose name combines the word for clarity and light with that for world. Her world, not just of desire but *of desire perfectly requited*, and of beauty perfectly realized,—here, a specifically literary *and* oneiric reality—is an intolerable menace to Sérapion and the Church and the logocentrism they embody, which depends on unambiguous distinctions, on reality and dream remaining distinct.

> *I could no longer distinguish the dream from the reality, nor could I discover where the reality began or where ended the dream. The exquisite young lord and libertine railed at the priest, the priest loathed the dissolute habits of the young lord. Two spirals entangled and confounded the one with the other, yet never touching, would afford a fair representation of this bicephalic life which I lived.*

Our selves are always multiplicitous and divided; for every positive desire, there are always simultaneously dissenting, opposite ones. Proust observed that in the course of our lives, we are many different people. Just as texts are never exactly the same at subsequent readings, and simultaneously reflect many different "meanings," so we are at any given moment inhabited by many different conventional realities, some of whom may be at odds. In Western psychology, the multiple self is usually considered an aberration, even an illness; Gautier's story attributes the same judgment to the Church. Freudian repression and (here) Catholic guilt are the means by which an illusion of integrity is forced on something essentially amorphous and multiple.

> Despite the strange character of my condition, I do not believe that I ever inclined, even for a moment, to madness [emphasis added]. *I always retained with extreme vividness all the perceptions of my two lives. Only there was one absurd fact which I could not explain to myself—namely, that the consciousness of the same individuality existed in two men so opposite in character. It was an anomaly for which I*

could not account—whether I believed myself to be the curé of the little village of C, or Il Signor Romualdo, the titled lover of Clarimonde.

    Be that as it may, I lived, at least I believed that I lived, in Venice. I have never been able to discover rightly how much of illusion and how much of reality there was in this fantastic adventure. We dwelt in a great palace on the Canaleio, filled with frescoes and statues, and containing two Titians in the noblest style of the great master, which were hung in Clarimonde's chamber. It was a palace well worthy of a king. We had each our gondola, our barcarolli *in family livery, our music hall, and our special poet. Clarimonde always lived upon a magnificent scale; there was something of Cleopatra in her nature. As for me, I had the retinue of a prince's son, and I was regarded with as much reverential respect as though I had been of the family of one of the twelve Apostles or the four Evangelists of the Most Serene Republic. I would not have turned aside to allow even the Doge to pass, and I do not believe that since Satan fell from heaven, any creature was ever prouder or more insolent than I. I went to the Ridotto, and played with a luck which seemed absolutely infernal. I received the best of all society—the sons of ruined families, women of the theatre, shrewd knaves, parasites, hectoring swashbucklers. But notwithstanding the dissipation of such a life, I always remained faithful to Clarimonde. I loved her wildly. She would have excited satiety itself, and chained inconstancy. To have Clarimonde was to have twenty mistresses; aye, to possess all women: so mobile, so varied of aspect, so fresh in new charms was she all in herself a very chameleon of a woman, in sooth.*

    Which is to say, she neither has nor conveys any sense of integrated self. Her multiplicity is infectious; it deconstructs the illusions of others. But from the perspective of the Church, what she does is create, not undo, illusions. These are two conventional realities about one phenomenon, two clashing modes of the same reality. Clarimonde, representing one, can inhabit the other without harm to herself, but it cannot tolerate her.

    She made you commit with her the infidelity you would have committed with another, by donning to perfection the character, the attraction, the style of beauty of the woman who appeared to please you. She returned my love a hundredfold, and it was in vain that the young patricians and even the Ancients of the Council of Ten made her the most magnificent proposals. A Foscari even went so far as to offer to espouse her. She rejected all

*his overtures. Of gold she had enough. She wished no longer for any-
thing but love—a love youthful, pure, evoked by herself, and which
should be a first and last passion. I would have been perfectly happy but
for a cursed nightmare which recurred every night, and in which I believed myself to be a poor village curé, practising mortification and penance for my excesses during the day.*

Romuald is haunted by the exigencies of the univocal self, "the
soul," an illusion to which he bound himself by the oaths of priesthood.

*Reassured by my constant association with her, I never thought further
of the strange manner in which I had become acquainted with Clarimonde. But the words of the Abbé Sérapion concerning her recurred
often to my memory, and never ceased to cause me uneasiness.*

*For some time the health of Clarimonde had not been so good as
usual; her complexion grew paler day by day. The physicians who were
summoned could not comprehend the nature of her malady and knew not
how to treat it. They all prescribed some insignificant remedies, and
never called a second time. Her paleness, nevertheless, visibly increased,
and she became colder and colder, until she seemed almost as white and
dead as upon that memorable night in the unknown castle. I grieved with
anguish unspeakable to behold her thus slowly perishing; and she,
touched by my agony, smiled upon me sweetly and sadly with the fateful
smile of those who feel that they must die.*

*One morning I was seated at her bedside, and breakfasting from a
little table placed close at hand, so that I might not be obliged to leave her
for a single instant. In the act of cutting some fruit I accidentally in-
flicted rather a deep gash on my finger. The blood immediately gushed
forth in a little purple jet, and a few drops spurted upon Clarimonde. Her
eyes flashed, her face suddenly assumed an expression of savage and ferocious joy such as I had never before observed in her. She leaped out of her
bed with animal agility—the agility, as it were, of an ape or a cat—*

Embracing the nonintegrity of the self means giving up any sense
of moral or spiritual superiority over animals, and admitting that they
share the same nature as we. To Sérapion, this is pagan, and monstrous.

*and sprang upon my wound, which she commenced to suck with an air
of unutterable pleasure. She swallowed the blood in little mouthfuls,*

slowly and carefully, like a connoisseur tasting a wine from Xeres or Sy-
racuse. Gradually her eyelids half closed, and the pupils of her green eyes
became oblong instead of round.

From time to time she paused in order to kiss my hand, then she
would recommence to press her lips to the lips of the wound

—in a kind of Sadian deconstruction of the physical self—her kisses
press proper, "natural" lips to man-made ones, extracting through a fis-
sure in the physical self the fluid most synonymous with its "life," and
taking it into herself as food—

in order to coax forth a few more ruddy drops.

When she found that the blood would no longer come, she arose
with eyes liquid and brilliant, rosier than a May dawn; her face full and
fresh, her hand warm and moist—in fine, more beautiful than ever, and
in the most perfect health.

"I shall not die! I shall not die!" she cried, clinging to my neck, half
mad with joy. "I can love thee yet for a long time. My life is thine, and all
that is of me comes from thee. A few drops of thy rich and noble blood,
more precious and more potent than all the elixirs of the earth, have
given me back life."

This scene long haunted my memory, and inspired me with
strange doubts in regard to Clarimonde; and the same evening, when
slumber had transported me to my presbytery, I beheld the Abbé Séra-
pion, graver and more anxious of aspect than ever. He gazed attentively
at me, and sorrowfully exclaimed: "Not content with losing your soul,
you now desire also to lose your body. Wretched young man, into how
terrible a plight have you fallen!" The tone in which he uttered these
words powerfully affected me, but in spite of its vividness even that im-
pression was soon dissipated, and a thousand other cares erased it from
my mind. At last one evening, while looking into a mirror whose traitor-
ous position she had not taken into account, I saw Clarimonde in the act
of emptying a powder into the cup of spiced wine which she had long
been in the habit of preparing after our repasts. I took the cup, feigned to
carry it to my lips, and then placed it on the nearest article of furniture as
though intending to finish it at my leisure. Taking advantage of a mo-
ment when the fair one's back was turned, I threw the contents under the
table, after which I retired to my chamber and went to bed, fully resolved

not to sleep, but to watch and discover what should come of all this mystery. I did not have to wait long. Clarimonde entered her nightdress, and having removed her apparel, crept into bed and lay down beside me. When she felt assured that I was asleep, she bared my arm, and drawing a gold pin from her hair, commenced to murmur in a low voice:

"One drop, only one drop! One ruby at the end of my needle. . . . Since thou lovest me yet, I must not die! . . . Ah, poor love! His beautiful blood, so brightly purple, I must drink it. Sleep, my only treasure! Sleep, my god, my child! I will do thee no harm; I will only take of thy life what I must to keep my own from being forever extinguished.

This might be an allegorical representation of what happens in every relation of genuine desire: there must always be some sense in which each party uses the other, physically and otherwise. The famous maxim of Chamfort, according to which "Love is merely the rubbing together of two bodies and the overlapping of two fantasies," interprets this kind of love cynically, from the traditional perpective of proscription, but the depiction here is not so negative. The text suggests that Romuald frequently avails himself sexually of Clarimonde's "essence"; here, she takes only a drop of his blood. Neither does the other the least harm, and both obtain enormous pleasure. But use of another is not condoned by the culture represented in the character of Sérapion, and today this might disparagingly be called "codependency."

But that I love thee so much, I could well resolve to have other lovers whose veins I could drain; but since I have known thee all other men have become hateful to me. . . . Ah, the beautiful arm! How round it is! How white it is! How shall I ever dare to prick this pretty blue vein!" And while thus murmuring to herself she wept, and I felt her tears raining on my arm as she clasped it with her hands. At last she took the resolve, slightly punctured me with her pin, and commenced to suck up the blood which oozed from the place. Although she swallowed only a few drops, the fear of weakening me soon seized her, and she carefully tied a little band around my arm, afterward rubbing the wound with an unguent which immediately cicatrized it.

Further doubts were impossible. The Abbé Sérapion was right. Notwithstanding this positive knowledge, however, I could not cease to love Clarimonde, and I would gladly of my own accord have given her all the blood she required to sustain her factitious life. Moreover, I felt but little fear of her. The woman seemed to plead with me for the vampire, and what I had already heard and seen sufficed to reassure me completely. In those days I had plenteous veins, which would not have been so easily exhausted as at present; and I would not have thought of bargaining for my blood, drop by drop. I would rather have opened myself the veins of my arm and said to her: "Drink, and may my love infiltrate itself throughout thy body together with my blood!" I carefully avoided ever making the least reference to the narcotic drink she had prepared for me, or to the incident of the pin, and we lived in the most perfect harmony.

Yet my priestly scruples commenced to torment me more than ever, and I was at a loss to imagine what new penance I could invent in order to mortify and subdue my flesh. Although these visions were involuntary, and though I did not actually participate in anything relating to them, I could not dare to touch the body of Christ with hands so impure and a mind defiled by such debauches whether real or imaginary. In the effort to avoid falling under the influence of these wearisome hallucinations, I strove to prevent myself from being overcome by sleep. I held my eyelids open with my fingers, and stood for hours together leaning upright against the wall, fighting sleep with all my might; but the dust of drowsiness invariably gathered upon my eyes at last, and finding all resistance useless, I would have to let my arms fall in the extremity of despairing weariness, and the current of slumber would again bear me away to the perfidious shores. Sérapion addressed me with the most vehement exhortations, severely reproaching me for my softness and want of fervor. Finally, one day when I was more wretched than usual, he said to me: "There is but one way by which you can obtain relief from this continual torment, and though it is an extreme measure it must be made use of; violent diseases require violent remedies. I know where Clarimonde is buried. It is necessary that we shall disinter her remains, and that you shall behold in how pitiable a state the object of your love is. Then you will no longer be tempted to lose your soul for the sake of an unclean corpse devoured by worms, and ready to crumble into dust. That will assuredly restore you to yourself."

Here, Buddhism and the "Catholicism" of Sérapion appear to find common ground. But there is still a difference: Sérapion would confine the "pitiable state" of "uncleanness" and death to Clarimonde, making of her a kind of scapegoat for death. The point of contemplation in the cremation grounds, for the Buddhist, is to realize that his or her own body is no different. This makes it difficult to attach overmuch metaphysical importance to the body, beautiful or not, but it is not necessarily intended to put an end to the pleasures of the flesh. Baudelaire's poems often seem torn between these two mutually exclusive treatments of death, just as Romuald is divided.

> For my part, I was so tired of this double life that I at once consented, desiring to ascertain beyond a doubt whether a priest or a gentleman had been the victim of delusion. I had become fully resolved either to kill one of the two men within me for the benefit of the other, or else to kill both, for so terrible an existence could not last long and be endured. The Abbé Sérapion provided himself with a mattock, a lever, and a lantern, and at midnight we wended our way to the cemetery of———, the location and place of which were perfectly familiar to him. After having directed the rays of the dark lantern upon the inscriptions of several tombs, we came at last upon a great slab, half concealed by huge weeds and devoured by mosses and parasitic plants, whereupon we deciphered the opening lines of the epitaph:

> > Here lies Clarimonde
> > Who was famed in her life-time
> > As the fairest of women.

> "It is here without a doubt," muttered Serapion, and placing his lantern on the ground, he forced the point of the lever under the edge of the stone and commenced to raise it. The stone yielded, and he proceeded to work with the mattock. Darker and more silent than the night itself, I stood by and watched him do it, while he, bending over his dismal toil, streamed with sweat, panted, and his hard-coming breath seemed to have the harsh tone of a death rattle. It was a weird scene, and had any persons from without beheld us, they would assuredly have taken us rather for profane wretches and shroud-stealers than for priests of God.

For are they not both at once? Priests and devils, as subservient to death as to their God? The irony and multiplicity embodied in Clarimonde are exemplified even by the character who hates them the most: Sérapion. In this scene, he, not Clarimonde, is repulsive and monstrous.

> There was something grim and fierce in Sérapion's zeal which lent him the air of a demon rather than of an apostle or an angel, and his great

aquiline face, with all its stern features brought out in strong relief by the lanternlight, had something fearsome in it which enhanced the unpleasant fancy. I felt an icy sweat come out upon my forehead in huge beads, and my hair stood up with a hideous fear. Within the depths of my own heart I felt that the act of the austere Sérapion was an abominable sacrilege; and I could have prayed that a triangle of fire would issue from the entrails of the dark clouds, heavily rolling above us, to reduce him to cinders. The owls which had been nestling in the cypress-trees, startled by the gleam of the lantern, flew against it from time to time, striking their dusty wings against its panes, and uttering plaintive cries of lamentation; wild foxes yelped in the far darkness, and a thousand sinister noises detached themselves from the silence. At last Sérapion's mattock struck the coffin itself, making its planks reecho with a deep sonorous sound, with that terrible sound nothingness utters when stricken. He wrenched apart and tore up the lid, and I beheld Clarimonde, pallid as a figure of marble, with hands joined; her white windingsheet made but one fold from her head to her feet. A little crimson drop sparkled like a speck of dew at one corner of her colorless mouth. Serapion, at this spectacle, burst into fury: "Ah, thou art here, demon! Impure courtesan! Drinker of blood and gold!" And he flung holy water upon the corpse and the coffin, over which he traced the sign of the cross with his sprinkler. Poor Clarimonde had no sooner been touched by the blessed spray than her beautiful body crumbled into dust, and became only a shapeless and frightful mass of cinders and half-calcined bones.

"Behold your mistress, my Lord Romuald!" cried the inexorable priest, as he pointed to these sad remains. "Will you be easily tempted after this to promenade on the Lido or at Fusina with your beauty?" I covered my face with my hands, a vast ruin had taken place within me. I returned to my presbytery, and the noble Lord Romuald, the lover of Clarimonde, separated himself from the poor priest with whom he had kept such strange company so long. But once only, the following night, I saw Clarimonde. She said to me, as she had said the first time at the portals of the church: "Unhappy man! Unhappy man! What hast thou done? Wherefore have hearkened to that imbecile priest? Wert thou not happy? And what harm had I ever done thee that thou shouldst violate my poor tomb, and lay bare the miseries of my nothingness? All communication between our souls and our bodies is henceforth forever broken. Adieu! Thou wilt yet regret me!" She vanished in air as smoke, and I never saw her more.

Alas! she spoke truly indeed. I have regretted her more than once, and I regret her still. My soul's peace has been very dearly bought. The love of God was not too much to replace such a love as hers. And this, brother, is the story of my youth. Never gaze upon a woman, and walk abroad only with eyes ever fixed upon the ground; for however chaste and watchful one may be, the error of a single moment is enough to make one lose eternity.

Clarimonde was the agent, engine, and embodiment of an artificial reality so powerful that it threatened to expose all realities as artificial. She threatened the hierarchy of meaning according to which every signifier has one proper signified, one referent, and every self is a static and homogeneous unity; according to which love and literature—the most accessible of artificial realities—must be kept in their place.

In his volume of Japanese ghost stories, *Kwaidan*, Hearn retold in English the story of *Yuki-Onna*, the snow woman, another beguiling female vampire. The protagonist of the story, a young woodcutter, finds himself stranded in a blizzard with an older man. They find shelter in an abandoned hut. In the middle of the night, the younger man awakens to see the life being drained from his friend by a beautiful female entity. She takes pity on him because, she tells him, he is young and pretty. But he must never tell anyone what he has seen, or she will find him and kill him. Later, he encounters a strange, beautiful girl on the road to Edo (Tokyo). He marries her, and she is a supernaturally perfect wife. After years together during which she keeps house and bears his children without showing any sign of age, he tells her what he saw in the hut that night, years before. "It was I," she tells him; she was the snow-woman. He betrayed her by telling the story she had forbidden him to tell to anyone, even his mother. She spares him only for the sake of their children, and disappears forever into the snowy winter night.

This story is similar in many ways to that of Clarimonde, but the differences between the two narratives may be more revealing than the resemblances. Instead of a life of passionate luxury, inexhaustible concupiscence, and satiety, the Japanese version presents a perfect vision of quiet domesticity. And Yuki is banished not by holy water, but by telling her the story about herself whose telling she had expressly forbidden. Telling the story collapses the apparent difference between Yuki the perfect, beautiful Japanese wife and mother, and the Snow Vampire. But they were always the same. Telling the story of what the woodcutter/husband saw in the hut merely reveals the absence of any distinction where one had been assumed to exist. Yuki could inhabit the day world of mortal men happily, harmlessly, only so long as her supernatural nature remained unnarrated, untold within that world. Her quite supernatural perfection, and that of her household, can only hold together for as long no clear distinction is asserted (by narrative) between the supernatural (reality) and the natural (illusion). That distinction goes unmade for years, and it is only finally made by accident. In an extraordinary irony, her husband betrays her by an act of supreme trust, telling her the one thing he has told no one ever. In an American ghost story, harboring such a secret, not revealing it, would probably be what exposed the protagonist to danger. The message is clear: the supernatural is not distinct from the natural until the distinction is named, narrated. Romuald also narrates that distinction, after Sérapion (or that part of him that is Sérapion) insists on it, and so cuts himself off forever from the perfect lover and the perfect life. Romuald does this because he allows himself to be persuaded by Sérapion that he cannot bear the "madness" of nondistinction, of multiplicity (although when "in" his multiplicitous state he says it did not feel like madness at all); his Japanese counterpart does so on the contrary quite by accident.

Japan for Hearn was the ultimate artificial reality—"elfish," "unreal"—and the perfect lover. In the landscape of Japan, he found himself living in a text like the one he had found in his aunt's library, depicting fauns, nymphs, and satyrs. He never woke up from this dream. Unlike the simple act of narration that turned Yuki back into Yuki-Onna, everything Hearn wrote after arriving in Japan blurred the distinction between real and imaginary, the perfect place of his imaginings and the real Japan where he was. Japan may be said to have taken the occasional drop of blood from him—it consumed him, body and mind; but like Clarimonde it gave him back so much more than it took. He never worried, as Romuald had, about being so many different people at once—the Greek, "Oriental" boy of his mother; Patrick, as his Irish aunt had called him; the American journalist; and finally Japanese, married to a Japanese woman, with Japanese children and a Japanese name. He tried to learn Japanese but never really succeeded, and spoke with his Japanese wife in a strange patois that she called "Mr. Hearn language." Forever exiled in his mind from his mother's tongue (Romaic), at the end of his life he found in Japanese, a language he never mastered, an instrument of reconciliation, the language of his imagination *because* he did not know it. It was his work as a writer to translate that incomprehensible perfection into English, which was always a *pis-aller* and therefore the epitome of all language, the practical instrument he used to reinvent himself, over and over. Hearn has the status of a kind of saint or demigod in Japan today; there is a museum in his honor, and the Japanese see him as a prophet who taught them to revere their own old ways, their own Japaneseness, even though this was something that he found in his own imaginings, and for which the physical Japan was only an ideal pretext.

He was able to do this because, in Japan, there was no Sérapion. The Buddhists he met were happy to collaborate in his imaginary affair with their country. His conversations with them appear again and again throughout his Japanese writings. They saw nothing wrong with his "Japanese" reinvention of himself, for which Buddhism offered an ideal epistemological grounding: "All things," he quoted a Buddhist proverb, "are merely dreams" (*In Ghostly Japan*, p. 169).

So in the sort of reversal which should seem usual by now, instead of this chapter being about Hearn, he turns out to have been about it. Instead of translating Gautier, it turns out that Hearn translated himself, as well as the last chapter of this book. And the texts have all read me—and you, for all that—as much as I have read them, or as I have read Hearn, or as Hearn read or wrote them. There is nothing in this phenomenon of narcissism or solipsism, for it reveals the Other, and the integrity of the self, as genial illusions, of practical value *sometimes*.

As every reader of poststructuralist theory knows, allegory ("a protracted metaphor") is defined by discontinuity with itself, always meaning something other than its apparent meaning: for example, the poem about love that never mentions love at all, but only talks about a rose that blooms and fades, or is "sick" from the worm that has found its heart (Blake). But here, in this reading, the subject, the reader, and the writer, are no less allegorical than the object, the text, each discontinuous with itself, each appearing to arise from the other.

In order not to be Sérapion, I will refrain from conclusions. This reading, and your reading of it, is only a street corner in the universe of possibilities, each of which is true, none relatively so. Like all happy coincidences, it has been both sought and unexpected, arbitrary, contingent, and absolutely necessary. Like the most fortuitous coincidences, of which life is full and which surprise only the young, this allegorical reading is both arbitrary and inevitable.

The priest Romuald need never have left his study to embrace the alterity represented by Clarimonde. No choice is necessary; the artificial distinction between good and evil, saint and whore, church and sin, breaks down on its own, into the most harmless and playful tension, and the name for it breaking down in Hearn/Gautier's story is Clarimonde, the world illumined by its own emptiness.

Having repressed, under Serapion's tutelage, his pleasant dream of emptiness, Romuald says that "What happened to me could not have happened in the natural order of things." And yet of course it did. The vision of Buddhism in this book arises, like Clarimonde, from within Sérapion's "Church," the imaginary edifice of Western literature and thought. It was there all the time. Nothing has moved; nothing has changed.

Notes

Introduction

1. See particularly Rorty's essay, "Inquiry as Recontextualization: An Antidualist Account of Interpretation," in which he says: "There is no self distinct from this self-reweaving web [of belief or habit of action]. All there is to human life is just that web" (p. 93). Rorty is also very close to Buddhist philosophy in insisting that there is no "relativism" implied by rejecting all possibility of a "general theory" or theories of "'interpretation' or 'knowledge' or 'truth' or 'meaning'" (p. 79).

2. Nishida Kitaro, Nishitani Keiji, and Abe Masao of the Kyoto School of Philosophy have argued for a Christian/Buddhist differentialism as well, relating the Christian concept of *kenosis* to *shunyata* or emptiness. From my perspective, their argument is fallacious, though it may in some instances have produced interesting results. I agree with Masao Abe that "In order for Christianity to become a world religion in the genuine sense, it must break through the limits of its present occidental form" (p. 266). *Kenosis* is from the Greek verb *kenoo*, meaning "I empty" (see Philippians 2.7: "[Christ] did not think to snatch at equality with God, but made himself nothing"); God is understood to have "emptied" himself in his incarnation as Jesus, assuming human limitations to which he would not otherwise have been subject. This has nothing whatever to do with Madhayamika or the Buddhist concept of emptiness, and in fact, insofar as it is synonymous with the doctrine of Incarnation, directly opposes the latter. The attempt to argue a connection between these quite diametrically opposed concepts is grounded, so far as I can tell, in nothing more than the similarity in literal meaning of the terms *kenosis* and *shunyata*, the common imputation of two kinds or levels of reality, and the fervent desire that a connection should exist.

3. Coward discusses the spiritual content of Derrida's work very precisely. It cannot be reduced to anything other than (in Derrida's own words) "transcendence beyond negativity" which "is *not accomplished by an intuition of a positive presence* [my emphasis] (Derrida, quoted in Coward, p. 158).

4. See Loy's *Nonduality: A Study in Comparative Philosophy*.

1. Proust and the Bonsai Tree

1. Reprinted in Gianfranco Giorgi, *Simon and Schuster's Guide to Bonsai*, pp. 15–18.

2. There is an adjective in Japanese, *natsukashii*, inadequately translated in bilingual dictionaries as "nostalgia-inducing" or "longed-for," which denotes a "Proustian" sense of nostalgia. Though having no equivalent in English, French, or any other Western language, it is a common word, heard in everyday use at all levels of expression. Any Japanese viewing maple leaves in the fall or cherry blossoms in spring—any natural phenomenon evocative of the passage of time and the cycle of seasons—might use it: "Natsukashii desu ne—" "Isn't this *natsukashii*?" The word perfectly reflects the Japanese sense of *reminding* as Kyuzo Murata means it, of nature, time, and mind as mutually evocative texts.

3. See *Japanese Arts and the Tea Ceremony*, pp. 29–38.

4. See J. Piggot, *Japanese Mythology*, and Stuart D. B. Picken, *Shinto*. In Buddhist epistemology, the sacred aspect of everyday reality, and of the natural, temporal world, is a function of emptiness and dependent arising (see chapter 2), and considerably more complex and subtle than the Shinto concept of *kami*.

5. See T. R. Reid, "Earth Spiders and Careful Tigers," for a popularized but well-informed discussion of these differences between Japan and the West.

6. I use this word guardedly. It must not be understood, as it usually is in the West, to imply theism, or mysticism. Buddhism is a genuine religion that is nontheistic and not essentially mystical.

7. See also Paul Davies, physicist:

> I cannot believe that our existence in this universe is a mere quirk of fate, an accident of history, an incidental blip in the great cosmic drama. Our involvement is too intimate. The physical species *Homo* may count for nothing, but the existence of mind in some organism on some planet in the universe is surely a fact of fundamental significance. Through conscious beings the universe has generated self-awareness. This can be no trivial detail, no minor byproduct of mindless purposeless forces. (*The Mind of God*, p. 232)

8. See Weisberg, et al., *Japonisme: Japanese Influence on French Art 1854–1910*; Richard Miles, *The Prints of Paul Jacoulet*.

9. See Picken, *Shinto*, p. 77: "One scholar has pointed out that if every shrine could be rebuilt every year, the ideal of renewal would be perfectly realized."

10. There are many other "Confucian" formulas throughout Proust's novel, such as "The Universe is true for all of us and dissimilar for each of us"; "One cannot cure suffering except by experiencing it fully"; "Every day I attach less importance to intelligence," and so on.

11. This *chi* is the basic principle of all traditional Chinese medicine, including acupuncture, and of *feng shui* (literally, "wind and water"), which has to do with the design and arrangement of houses, furniture, gardens, and so forth to achieve and maintain harmony between the human and the natural flow of *chi*. See Sara Rossbach, *Feng-Shui: The Chinese Art of Placement*.

12. See my *The Otherness Within*.

2. Reading Emptiness

1. Contemporary scholars agree that there were several Nagarjunas. The original one lived during the second to third centuries A.D., and only three works are attributed to him with any certainty (the work cited here is not one of them). There are, moreover, several schools of thought within the Indo-Tibetan Madhymika system. The view of the Middle Way presented here is mostly that of the "Middle Way Consequence," or Madhyamika-Prasangika School, which long ago came to dominate Tibetan Buddhist epistemology *(abidharma)*, according to which all phenomena arise and exist in a state of mutual interdependence, so that none can be said to have any being independent of the others, and all are said to be "empty."

2. This text, though attributed to the founder of Zen Buddhism, was almost certainly not written by him.

3. In *The Otherness Within* (Baton Rouge: LSU Press, 1983).

4. Robert Magliola has written about the striking structural and semantic resemblances between Derrida and Nagarjuna: "Nagarjuna takes as his specific task the deconstruction of the principle of identity; and to accomplish this, he employs the same logical strategy, and often the very same arguments, as Derrida" (*Derrida on the Mend*, p. 88). Less convincingly, Magliola divides the various schools of Buddhist philosophy into "logocentric" and "differential," imposing criteria derived from deconstruction onto Buddhist thought rather than letting each inform the other. This, to me, departs from the Middle Way. Magliola relies on D. T. Suzuki in presenting Madhyamika as "differential," therefore "good" Buddhist thought, and Yogacara (Mind-Only) as logocentric. This would seem to be a serious misconstrual of Yogacara. (See Faure, 224–25.) Faure suggests that Magliola might place a figure like Dogen on the logocentric

side, where he clearly does not belong. Instead, my readings suggest that there is an essentialist and a "differential" aspect in every thought or mode of thought. To suggest that these could be sorted out neatly is quite counter to the Middle Way as I understand it.

3. The Karmic Text

1. The Gelukba—or Gelukpa or Gelugpa, meaning "school of the virtuous" in Tibetan—is one of the four great schools of Tibetan Buddhism, the last founded (by Tsong Khapa in the fourteenth century). The Dalai Llama is leader of the Gelukbas, who through him wield political as well as spiritual leadership. The Gelukbas are known for their emphasis on the rules of monastic order, and scholasticism, the study of Buddhist literature and philosophy.

2. See J. Derrida, "Differance," *Margins of Philosophy*: "Since Being has never had a 'meaning,' has never been thought or said as such, except by dissimulating itself in beings, then differance, in a certain and very strange way, (is) 'older' than the ontological difference or than the truth of Being. When it has this age it can be called the play of the trace. The play of a trace which no longer belongs to the horizon of Being, but whose play transports and encloses the meaning of Being: the play of the trace, or the différance, which has no meaning, and is not" (22).

3. Thurman wishes to conflate the Buddhist position with that of analytic philosophy. I part company with him on this, though it may be true in specific instances. I remain convinced that deconstruction is closer to Buddhist philosophy, despite its absolutist tendency (the tendency to become an absolutist skepticism).

4. There can be several justifications for difficulty, according to Buddhist thought. in the first, if concepts are subtle and complex, even the clearest exposition may be difficult. In the second, a certain degree of opacity may be required to cloak esoteric teachings from those who are not ready to receive them, and to assure that the practitioner's progress is supervised by a qualified teacher (guru). In this case understanding requires that a text be "unlocked" by a master, who integrates the root text with its commentary for the student. In the third, difficulty itself may accomplish a desired end, perhaps to help readers/practitioners "break free from the deadened dependency on literal language," or to "overcome their habitual addiction to ordinariness of conception and perception" (Thurman 1988, pp. 138–39). Particularly in tantric texts, which can be very poetic and beautiful, "literary" in the Western sense, "clarity was not necessarily the main thing. . . . Sometimes a disciple would need his clarity shattered, his intellectual control of reality shaken by the deliberate introduc-

tion of obscurity. And often the vajra guru spoke in riddles or symbolically, cultivating a special type of discourse known (controversially) as 'twilight language' . . ." (Thurman 1988, p. 126). These are the justified instances of difficulty. The last is a form of charlatanism: difficulty for its own sake, or for the purposes of intellectual self-aggrandizement. Unfortunately, all of the justifiable uses of difficulty involve significant risk of degenerating into the latter, by force of habit if nothing else.

Derrida's early writings (including *Of Grammatology*) were certainly a case of justifiable—inevitable—difficulty. I am not so sure that this is still true. In de Man's work, there is a strong sense of opacity (as well as the insistence on epistemological failure) deployed to a specific pedagogical end, though it is doubtful whether this is always the case. Unfortunately, difficulty connotes power in much of Western academic tradition.

5. My evocation of mantra here is somewhat idiosyncratic. *Mantra*—Sanskrit for "thinking instrument," instrument for thinking—sacred incantation, is a special case of language with its own theoretical basis in Buddhist thought. It reflects the idea prevalent in esoteric Buddhism, for instance in the Shingon (Japanese for "truth word") sect of Japan, that "foundationally (that is, at the subperceptible level) every word is a true word *(shingon)* in that it is a surface (macrocosmic) manifestation of a microcosmic expression within Dainichi [Vairochana Buddha]'s enlightened activity. . . . through mantric practice, one knows directly the truth words *(shingon)* inaudible to ordinary hearing," which invest all language (Kasulis 1988, pp. 262–63).

4. The Dream of Buddhist Japan

1. See Julian Symons's biography of Poe, *The Tell-Tale Heart*, p. 177.

2. See Carl Dawson, *Lafcadio Hearn and the Vision of Japan*: "Of course [Hearn] described 'a fictive nation,' in Roland Barthes's words, a faraway system of his own realizing, which Hearn, the chronic namer, called 'Japan'" (p. 157).

3. See note 5, chapter 3.

Bibliography

Aitken, Robert. *Encouraging Words. Zen Buddhist Teachings for Western Students.* New York and San Francisco: Pantheon, 1993.

———. *Taking the Path of Zen.* New York: Farrar Straus, Giroux/North Point Press, 1982.

Bankei. *The Unborn. The Life and Teachings of Zen Master Bankei (1622–1693).* Trans. Norman Waddell. San Francisco: North Point Press, 1984.

Barnstone, Willis. *The Poetics of Translation. History, Theory, Practice.* New Haven: Yale University Press, 1993.

Barthes, Roland. *The Empire of Signs.* Trans. Richard Howard. New York: Hill and Wang, 1982.

Bassui. *Mud and Water.* Trans. Arthur Braverman. San Francisco: North Point Press, 1989.

Benjamin, Walter. "The Task of the Translator." *Illuminations,* 69–82. New York: Schocken Books, 1969.

Biguenet, John, and Schulte, Rainer. *The Craft of Translation.* Chicago: University of Chicago Press, 1989.

Blanchot, Maurice. *Le livre à venir.* Paris: Gallimard, 1959.

Bodhidharma. *The Zen Teachings of Bodhidharma.* Ed. and trans. Red Pine. New York: Farrar Straus, Giroux/North Point Press, 1987.

Brockhaus, Albert. *Netsukes.* Reprint. New York: Hacker Art Books, 1975.

Cabezon, Jose-Ignacio. *Buddhism and Language. A Study of Indo-Tibetan Scholasticism.* Albany: SUNY Press, 1994.

Chandrakirti. "The Entry into the Middle Way." In C. W. Huntington, Jr., and Geshe Namgyal Wangchen. *The Emptiness of Emptiness. An Introduction to Early Indian Madhyamika.* Honolulu: University of Hawaii Press, 1989. 145–98.

Chu-Tsing Li. "The Artistic Theories of the Literati." *The Chinese Scholar's Studio:*

Artistic Life in the Late Ming Period, 14–22. Ed. Chu-Tsing Li and James C. Y. Watt. London: Thames and Hudson, 1987.

Cleary, Thomas. *Entry Into the Inconceivable: An Introduction to Hua-Yen Buddhism*. Honolulu: University of Hawaii Press, 1983.

Confucious. *The Essential Confucious*. Trans. Thomas Cleary. San Francisco: HarperSanFrancisco, 1992.

Cott, Jonathan. *Wandering Ghost: the Odyssey of Lafcadio Hearn*. New York: Knopf, 1991.

Coward, Harold. *Derrida and Indian Philosophy*. Albany: SUNY Press, 1990.

David-Neel, Alexandra. *Magic and Mystery in Tibet*. Reprint. New York: Dover, 1971.

———. *The Secret Oral Teachings in Tibetan Buddhist Sects*. San Francisco: City Lights Books, 1967.

Davies, Paul. *The Mind of God: The Scientific Basis for a Rational Universe*. New York: Simon and Schuster, 1992.

Dawson, Carl. *Lafcadio Hearn and the Vision of Japan*. Baltimore: Johns Hopkins University Press, 1992.

de Man, Paul. *Allegories of Reading*. New Haven: Yale University Press, 1979.

———. *The Resistance to Theory*. Minneapolis: University of Minnesota Press, 1986.

Derrida, Jacques. *De la grammatologie*. Paris: Les Editions de minuit, 1967.

———. *Derrida and Chinese Philosophy*. Special Issue of the *Journal of Chinese Philosophy* 17:1 (March 1990).

Dogen. *Rational Zen: The Mind of Dogen Zenji*. Ed. and trans. Thomas Cleary. Boston: Shambala, 1993.

———. *Shobogenzo-zuimonki: Sayings of Eihei Dogen Zenji recorded by Koun Ejo*. Trans. Shohaku Okumura. Kyoto: Kyoto Soto-Zen Center, 1987.

Dowman, Keith, ed. and trans. *The Flight of the Garuda. Teachings of the Dzokchen Tradition of Tibetan Buddhism*. Boston: Wisdom, 1994.

Encyclopedia of Japan. Tokyo and New York: Kodansha, 1993.

Faure, Bernard. *Chan Insights and Oversights. An Epistemological Critique of the Chan Tradition*. Princeton: Princeton University Press, 1993.

Flaubert, Gustave. *Oeuvres* vols. I and II. Paris: Bibliothèque de la Pléiade, 1952.

Graham, Joseph, ed. *Difference in Translation*. Ithaca: Cornell University Press, 1985.

Granet, Marcel. *La pensée chinoise*. Paris: Albin Michel, 1968.

Griffin, Donald R. *Animal Minds*. Chicago: University of Chicago Press, 1992.

Guenther, Herbert V., and Kawamura, Leslie S., eds. and trans. *Mind in Buddhist Psychology. A Translation of Ye-shes rgyal-mtshan's "The Necklace of Clear Understanding."* Berkeley, Calif.: Dharma Publishing, 1975.

Gyatso, Geshe Kelsang. *Buddhism in the Tibetan Tradition*. Trans. Tenzin P. Phunrabpa. London and New York: Arkana, 1988.

Hawking, Stephen W. *A Brief History of Time*. New York: Bantam, 1988.

Hearn, Lafcadio. "By Force of Karma." *Kokoro: Hints and Echoes of Japanese Inner Life*, 155–69. Reprint. Rutland and Tokyo: Tuttle, 1972.

———. *Essays in European and Oriental Literature*. New York: Dodd, Mead, 1923.

———. *Exotics and Retrospectives*. Reprint. Upper Saddle River, N.J.: Literature House/Gregg Press, 1969.

———. *Glimpses of Unfamiliar Japan*. Reprint. Rutland and Tokyo: Tuttle, 1976.

———. *In Ghostly Japan*. Reprint. Rutland and Tokyo: Tuttle, 1971.

———. *Kwaidan: Stories and Studies of Strange Things*. Reprint. New York: Dover, 1968.

———. *Life and Letters*, vol. I. Ed. Elizabeth Bisland. Boston: Houghton Mifflin/The Riverside Press Cambridge, 1923.

———. "Nirvana." *Gleanings in Buddha Fields. Studies of Hand and Soul in the Far East*, 211–66. Boston and New York: Houghton Mifflin, 1897.

———. trans. *One of Cleopatra's Nights and Other Fantastic Romances by Théophile Gautier*. New York: R. Worthington, 1882.

Heine, Steven. *Dogen and the Koan Tradition. A Tale of Two Shobogenzo Texts*. Albany: SUNY Press, 1994.

Hopkins, Jeffrey. *Emptiness Yoga*. Ithaca: Snow Lion, 1987.

——— and Tenzin Gyatso (the Dalai Lama). *Kalachakra Tantra Rite of Initiation*. Rev. ed. London: Wisdom Publications, 1989.

———. *Meditation on Emptiness*. London: Wisdom, 1983.

Humphries, Jefferson. "Montaigne's Anti-Influential Model of Identity." *Losing the Text: Readings in Literary Desire*, 3–20. Athens: University of Georgia Press, 1986.

———. *The Otherness Within: Gnostic Readings in Marcel Proust, Flannery O'Connor, and Francois Villon*. Baton Rouge: LSU Press, 1983.

Huntington, C. W. See Chandrakirti.

Huysmans, Joris-Karl. *A rebours*. Paris: Garnier-Flammarion, 1978.

Ives, Colta Feller. *The Great Wave: The Influence of Japanese Woodcuts on French Prints*. New York: Metropolitan Museum of Art/New York Graphic Society, 1974.

Japanese Arts and the Tea Ceremony. trans. Joseph P. MacAdam. New York and Tokyo: Weatherhill/Heibonsha, 1974.

Jullien, Francois. "L'Oeuvre et l'univers: Imitation ou déploiement (Limites à une conception mimetique de la création littéraire dans la tradition chinoise)." *Extrême-Orient, Extrême-Occident* 1984, 3: 37–88.

———. *Procès ou création: Une introduction à la pensée des lettres chinoises*. Paris: Editions du Seuil, 1989.

Kafka, Franz. *The Great Wall of China*. New York: Schocken Books, 1970.

Kalupahana, David J. See Nagarjuna.

Kasulis, Thomas P. "Truth Words: The Basis of Kukai's Theory of Interpretation," 257–72. *Buddhist Hermeneutics*. Ed. Donald S. Lopez, Jr. Honolulu: University of Hawaii Press, 1988.

———. "The Incomparable Philosopher: Dogen on How to Read the *Shobogenzo*." *Dogen Studies*, 83–98. Ed. William R. LaFleur. Honolulu: University of Hawaii Press, 1985.

Kim, Hee-Jin. *Dogen Kigen: Mystical Realist*. Tucson: University of Arizona Press, 1987.

Klein, Ann. *Knowledge and Liberation. Tibetan Buddhist Epistemology in Support of Transformative Religious Experience*. Ithaca: Snow Lion, 1986.

Kyuzo Murata. Untitled essay. Gianfranco Giorgi. *Simon and Schuster's Guide to Bonsai*, 15–18. Ed. Victoria Jahn. New York: Simon and Schuster, 1990.

Lanier, Jaron. "Comparative Illusions: Jaron Lanier on the Potential of Virtual Reality." *Tricycle* Summer 1994 (III:4). 57.

Lao-Tzu. *The Essential Tao*. Trans. Thomas Cleary. San Francisco: HarperSan-Francisco, 1992.

Lautréamont. *Oeuvres complètes*. Paris: NRF/Gallimard, 1973.

Loy, David. *Nonduality: A Study in Comparative Philosophy*. New Haven: Yale University Press, 1988.

Magliola, Robert. *Derrida on the Mend*. West Lafayette, Indiana: Purdue University Press, 1984.

————. "Differentialism in Chinese *Ch'an* and French Deconstruction: Some Test-Cases from the Wu-Men-Kuan." *Journal of Chinese Philosophy* 17:1 (March 1990) 87–97.

Merrill, James. *Divine Comedies*. New York: Atheneum, 1976.

————. *Recitative*. San Francisco: North Point Press, 1986.

Miles, Richard. *The Prints of Paul Jacoulet*. London: Robert G. Sawers Publishing/Pacific Asia Museum, 1982.

Montaigne, Michel de. *Oeuvres completes*. Ed. A. Thibaudet and M. Rat. Paris: Bibliothèque de la Pléiade, 1962.

Morse, Edward S. *Japanese Homes and their Surroundings*. Reprint. New York. Dover, 1961.

Muso Soseki. *Sun at Midnight: Poems and Sermons*. Trans. W. S. Merwin and Soiku Shigematsu. San Francisco: North Point Press, 1989.

Nagarjuna. *Master of Wisdom. Writings of the Buddhist Master Nagarjuna*. Trans. and ed. Chr. Lindtner. Berkeley, Calif.: Dharma Publishing, 1986. [Referred to as Nagarjuna.]

————. *The Philosophy of the Middle Way*. Ed. and trans. David J. Kalupahana. Albany: SUNY Press, 1986. [Referred to as Nagarjuna, *Philosophy*.]

Napper, Elizabeth. *Dependent Arising and Emptiness*. London: Wisdom, 1989.

————, ed. and trans., and Lati Rinbochay. *Mind in Tibetan Buddhism*. Ithaca: Snow Lion, 1980.

O'Connor, Flannery. *A Good Man Is Hard to Find, And Other Stories*. New York: Harcourt, Brace, Jovanovich, 1976.

Pabongka Rinpoche. *Liberation in the Palm of Your Hand*. Rev. ed. Ed. Trijang Rinpoche, trans. Michael Richards. Boston: Wisdom Publications, 1993.

Penrose, Roger. *The Emperor's New Mind.* Oxford and New York: Oxford University Press, 1989.

Picken, Stuart D. B. *Shinto: Japan's Spiritual Roots.* Tokyo and New York: Kodansha, 1980.

Piggott, Juliet. *Japanese Mythology.* London: Paul Hamlyn, 1969.

Proust, Marcel. *A la recherche du temps perdu.* 3 vols. Paris: Bibliothèque de la Pléiade, 1954.

Reid, T. R. "Earth Spiders and Careful Tigers." *International Wildlife* March–April 1992 (22:2), 40–47.

Reynolds, John Myrdhin. ed. and trans. *Self-Liberation Through Seeing with Naked Awareness.* Barrytown, New York: Station Hill Press, 1989.

Rorty, Richard. *Objectivity, Relativism, and Truth: Philosophical Papers, Vol. I.* Cambridge: Cambridge University Press, 1991.

Rosenfield, Israel. *The Strange, Familiar and Forgotten: An Anatomy of Consciousness.* New York: Knopf, 1992.

Rossbach, Sarah. *Feng-Shui: the Chinese Art of Placement.* London and New York: Arkana, 1991.

Sopa, Geshe Lhundup, and Jeffrey Hopkins. *Cutting Through Appearances. Practice and Theory of Tibetan Buddhism.* Ithaca: Snow Lion, 1989.

Stein, Rolf A. *The World in Miniature: Container Gardens and Dwellings in Far Eastern Religious Thought.* Trans. Phyllis Brooks. Stanford: Stanford University Press, 1990.

Suzuki, Takao. *Words in Context: A Japanese Perspective on Language and Culture.* Tokyo and New York: Kodansha, 1984.

Takahashi, Masanobu. *The Essence of Dogen.* London: Kegan Paul International, 1983.

Thurman, Robert A. F. *The Central Philosophy of Tibet. A Study and Translation of Jey Tsong Khapa's* Essence of True Eloquence. Princeton: Princeton University Press, 1984.

———. "Vajra Hermeneutics." *Buddhist Hermeneutics,* 119–48. Ed. Donald S. Lopez, Jr. Honolulu: University of Hawaii Press, 1988.

Wallace, B. Alan. *Choosing Reality. A Comtemplative View of Physics and the Mind.* Boston: Shambala, 1989.

Watts, Alan. *Om: Creative Meditations*. Ed. Judith Johnstone. Berkeley: Creative Arts, 1980.

Weisberg, Gabriel P., et al. *Japonisme: Japanese Influence on French Art 1854–1910*. Cleveland: Cleveland Museum of Art, 1975.

White Lotus: An Introduction to Tibetan Culture. Ed. Carole Eichert. Ithaca: Snow Lion, 1990.

Yeshe, Lama. *The Tantric Path of Purification*. Boston: Wisdom Publications, 1995.

Yoshida, Kenichi. *Japan is a Circle*. Tokyo, New York, and San Francisco: Kodansha, 1981.

Zen Flesh, Zen Bones: A Collection of Zen and Pre-Zen Writings. Ed. Paul Reps. Rutland, Vermont and Tokyo: Tuttle, 1957.

Zimmerman, Michael. "Heidegger, Buddhism, and Deep Ecology." Charles Guignon, ed., *The Cambridge Companion to Heidegger*, 240–69. Cambridge: Cambridge University Press, 1993.

Zolbrod, Leon. Introduction to Ueda Akinari, *"Ugetsu Monogatari": Tales of Moonlight and Rain*, 19–94. Rutland, Vermont, and Tokyo: Tuttle, 1977.

Index